The Mainstreaming Handbook

HOW TO BE AN ADVOCATE FOR
YOUR SPECIAL-NEEDS STUDENTS

Deborah Coughlin

HEINEMANN
Portsmouth, NH

To Karen:
the heart, soul, and inspiration behind this book.
Your spirit continuously reminds me to be a better person and teacher.
I love you and admire you.
Thank you for being my friend.

Heinemann
A division of Reed Elsevier Inc.
361 Hanover Street
Portsmouth, NH 03801–3912
www.heinemann.com

Offices and agents throughout the world

Library of Congress Cataloging-in-Publication Data
Coughlin, Deborah.
   The mainstreaming handbook : how to be an advocate for your special-needs students /
Deborah Coughlin ; [editor, Lois Bridges].
      p. cm.
   Includes bibliographical references and index.
   ISBN 0-325-00226-6
      1. Mainstreaming in education—United States—Case studies. 2. Handicapped
   children—Education (Elementary)—United States—Case studies. 3. Handicapped
   children—Legal status, laws, etc.—United States.   I. Bird, Lois Bridges.   II. Title.
   LC1201.C68 2000
   371.9′046—dc21   99-055088

Editor: Lois Bridges
Production: Reuben Kantor
Cover design: Jenny Jensen Greenleaf
Manufacturing: Louise Richardson

Printed in the United States of America on acid-free paper
04 03 02 01 00 DA 1 2 3 4 5

Contents

4

Understanding Literacy and Learning   71

5

Karen: A Portrait of a Special Needs Student   85

6

A Classroom Literacy Program for All Students   113

Acknowledgments

I would like to thank my editor Lois Bridges. You have an incredible talent and patience for looking at my first drafts and finding the focus. Thank you for truly supporting and nurturing me through this learning experience.

And a special thank you to my husband, Daniel. Your proofreading, feedback, and knowledge of classroom teaching were invaluable to me. The fact that you tended to yourself and didn't complain about being ignored also helped tremendously. Thank you.

1

What Is Mainstreaming?

I am an elementary classroom teacher at a year-round magnet school in Florida. In the past ten years, I have been the regular classroom teacher for students whose situations are believed to interfere with academic learning. The circumstances of these children include:

- Attention Deficit Disorder (ADD)
- Attention Deficit Hyperactivity Disorder (ADHD)
- multiple physical and mental handicaps[1]
- cerebral palsy
- asthma
- brain cancer
- leukemia
- allergies
- hearing aids
- Title 1 attendance
- English as a second language
- gifted
- standardized IQ scores are between 69 and 140
- Educable Mentally Handicapped (EMH)
- learning disabled and gifted
- Spanish speaking only
- Vietnamese speaking only
- learning disabled
- speech difficulties
- severe vision loss or physical problems involving movement of the eyes

Many children in my classroom were experiencing difficulties in their personal lives that surely affected their performance and learning in school. These children also had special needs and included:

- a child from Cambodia who spent time with his family in refugee camps. He wrote of eating rats and watching his friends being mowed down by gunfire while playing tag in the streets at Christmas
- a child whose older brother was recently abducted, raped, and murdered while playing after school
- a child who chose not to speak due to trauma
- a child who was occasionally committed to local mental health institutions for three-day observations
- a child who lived in a car
- a child whose grandfather and uncle went to Mexico on vacation and never returned. Their vehicle, when located, was burned and ransacked. After a year, the bodies were still not found.
- a child who was said to masturbate on chairs during lessons
- a child who frequently described his school supplies, treats, and toys as being stolen by his parents on family shopping outings
- numerous children whose parents were in various stages of separation and divorce
- children of sexual abuse
- children of physical abuse
- children that were hungry
- children whose parents were arrested the evening before and were still in jail
- children in foster or state care
- children whose parents were beaten up
- children whose parents were in jail long term
- children whose parents openly prostitute
- children whose parents openly use and/or sell drugs
- children who don't know where their parents are
- children raised by grandparents
- children whose parents expose them to sexually inappropriate materials
- children who live with their mother and one or more uncles

- children whose parents were unemployed
- children who were physically dirty
- children who were not cared for medically

Few of these children qualify for special services within the school system. However, all of the children with physical conditions qualify for special education services if their condition meets the federal criteria for a handicap and their disabling condition is documented by medical doctors as interfering with their learning. The children who are considered learning disabled and gifted also receive special education services. Those children performing below expectations academically, but do not have a handicap as defined by the law, may qualify for Title 1 services depending upon the school that they attend and their federal eligibility criteria.

Beginning with the Rehabilitation Act of 1973, there has been a dramatic increase of children deemed as having special needs that have been mainstreamed and/or placed as full inclusion students in a regular classroom setting. In 1990, the National Joint Committee on Learning Disabilities reported that more than 90 percent of students with disabilities are taught in the regular classroom for some part of their school day. Today, with the recent update in federal laws, there is an increased burden on school districts to justify a noninclusive placement. Funding restrictions have been eased and reorganized, and no longer are there financial incentives for placing children with disabilities in separate classrooms. In fact, school districts are now required to explain in writing why they are not offering the child with disabilities a placement in the regular classroom. Regular classroom teachers are in the precarious position of learning how to accommodate children with special needs through the trial and error of immersion. It's a very unsettling feeling working with children and wondering if your personal best is good enough. Never having been trained in the field of special education and encountering these issues as a beginning teacher was beyond my realm of competencies, preparation, priorities, and expectations.

During my first year of teaching, I had a first grade class at a school where administrators met over the summer and placed the entire student body into their assigned reading and math groups for the next school year. The children were organized into groups based upon the results of their end-of-the-year standardized tests. Students in every classroom were then listed by their scores numerically from highest to lowest. The top third of each class became the high group, the middle third the average group, and the lower third the low group. Obviously, teacher decision had been removed from the equation, and at that point in my career, I was grateful for the support and pleased with the initiative of the school administrators.

Throughout the year, I did everything I was supposed to do, right down the line. I scheduled my curriculum according to all of the textbook teacher editions, the district guidelines, and most importantly, where my fellow first grade teachers were in their curriculum. By September, I had mastered the scheduling routine. In reading, we completed one story a week from the basal using most of the accompanying worksheets as seatwork. In the phonics workbook, we completed one page a day together as a class. In math, I scheduled one page that we did in class together and one page that the children took home or completed independently. I got so proficient at this routine that by February I had all of my plans written in my plan book for the remainder of the school year. All I needed to do was to pull my respective worksheets, create some fillers for centers, and I was done. I felt really good about that.

Not long into that school year however, I began to notice some things that didn't make sense to me. I was confused by my reading groups. I had all three reading groups meeting daily and I was following what the teacher's manual and the other teachers said to do, but it seemed senseless to me after a while. First, I noticed that I had to work diligently to maintain the integrity of these three different groups set up by the administrators. All three groups (high, medium, and low) were using the same reading series and frequently using the same basal book simultaneously. Regardless of which group I worked with, my actual lessons remained the same. The only difference between my reading groups was how fast we covered the material—not the manner in which I taught it. Pace and students' location in the book were of major importance to the school. It was imperative that I keep each group working about two weeks behind each other.

This was difficult because my second realization and puzzlement was that many of the children in my lower two groups were actually better readers than the children in my higher group. By better readers I mean that they could pick up their reading series and actually read a story to me. Several of my higher reading group students were not reading print in context. On many occasions, I actually slowed down the progress of my lower groups to accommodate the children who were unable to read in the higher group. Eventually, I found myself spending more time with my higher group simply to keep them moving and to maintain the integrity of the schedule, while the children in the lower groups spent more time at centers and reading books independently or with friends.

Wondering how these students could be considered my high ability reading group weighed heavily on my mind. Yet, almost all of their worksheets and official evaluations qualified them for As in reading and therefore As on their report cards. They completed all of their weekly sight word lists competently and scored highly on all standardized measures. On paper, these children looked like efficient, strong readers. Yet, when these very same children were handed the textbook that those sight words or assessments came from, they were unable to read the story accurately or fluently,[2] or produce a retelling of the story in any verbal or printed form.

On the other hand, my little "nonreaders" were failing (or misplacing) most of their assessments. Based on their printed work, I found myself giving reading report card grades of Cs and Ds to children who could truly read a book; and I was giving As to children who could not. It just didn't seem to make sense. I knew I was doing everything I was told to do, but was concerned and confused by the fact that some children were being misrepresented. It was difficult to explain how a child could fail reading if they could read, and get an A if they couldn't. I just didn't get it. It was certainly clear to me that I needed to know more about what I was doing.

During this first year of teaching, my children believed to have special needs left the classroom for reading and math instruction. The school did not have a special education program that I was aware of. The students left to attend a program called Chapter 1 (now known as Title 1). They were usually gone until lunchtime. I never spoke with the person who picked them up each day, nor did I ever know her name. At that time, I assumed Chapter 1 to be a program for the economically poor because all of the children who left my room were on free or reduced lunch, and most of them came to school dirty and unkempt. They were all predominately children of color and mostly boys. Each day they were removed from the classroom by a teaching assistant who I remember only because she wore pale-blue bedroom slippers to school every day. It was my assumption that the program was similar to the Head Start concept. Nobody ever discussed the program with me. The only thing I knew for sure was that they went somewhere else for reading and math and I didn't need to prepare for them or worry about them. Actually, I had four groups of children: the high, the medium, the low, and the children who left.

One of the children who left my class was Ben. Ben was six. He was of African American descent and lived in a reportedly heavy crime area, which was referred to as Little Vietnam. Weapons, drugs, and prostitution were the norm in Ben's neighborhood. He rarely spoke, and when he did, he almost mumbled. He had six brothers and sisters, and his left eye would wander off in the direction of his left ear when he chose to make eye contact. Ben was considered a nonreader. Actually, I think he may have been considered a non everything. In school, the kids were either picking on him or ignoring him. Outside of school, it was reported that he was the scapegoat for his siblings, parents, and the neighborhood kids. By the time Ben arrived at school in the morning, he was usually agitated or despondent. He seemed to work very hard in class when he was able to focus and responded well to praise.

Ben came to school one day with a word in his head that he said he knew. The word was "food," and to prove it he was going to write it on the blackboard. After announcing this to the class, Ben quickly and awkwardly scratched the letters P- U- b- l- i- X on the blackboard. He turned to his classmates and grinned. Publix is the name of a popular local supermarket chain in the southeast. Of course most of the children recognized the word and laughed at Ben. Knowing as little as I did about establishing a classroom community, as well as not understanding literacies, it still seemed to me that what Ben had just demonstrated was a strength, not a weakness. I saw desire and promise.

Ben began to bring words from home to read. He would rip them out of magazines or find them in flyers. He'd bring in items, such as McDonald's french fry bags that he found on the sidewalk. When I finished with the other children and had some time, Ben and I would look for words after he returned from his Chapter 1 classes. Ben, as well as that entire year, filled me with questions.

It was obvious that I did not have the experience or knowledge to participate equally or comfortably in discussions regarding the competencies or literacies of my students: regular or special education. In fact, I wasn't even aware that I should be participating in discussions that pertained to the academic placement of my children in the classroom. It never occurred to me to intervene or involve myself in what I considered administrative or special education issues. I was more than compliant and open to accommodating the needs of administrators and special education students in my classroom. I just needed somebody to tell me how, when, and what to do. It is my consideration that every mainstreamed child affects at least twenty other students. Accommodating their needs is a requirement, a concern, and a lot of work.

By retracing my own processes and questions during my years of teaching, I describe in this book the procedures and special investigations that I encountered in my search to advocate for and accommodate special needs students in the regular classroom. These inquiries educated me to the laws, procedures, and politics involved when working with all students in my classroom. My inquiries allowed me to come to my own understandings and adjustments when accommodating various needs in my classroom. By demystifying and deconstructing the field of special education and literacy, a new confidence and ownership occurred. With knowledge came a sense of control, voice, and participation.

It is my hope that this book will address and answer most of the issues, questions, and concerns pertinent to special education services, mainstreaming, inclusion, children labeled at risk, and Title 1. Although it is written primarily as a guide to assist the general elementary teacher, the information pertains to parents, administrators, secondary educators, and child advocates as well. Chapter 2 introduces you to the nuts and bolts of the federal programs you should know. These laws were established in July of 1997 and implemented in July of 1998.

Chapter 3 looks at how the federal laws are applied in our classrooms. We address the most common questions, issues, and concerns that arise while accommodating and supporting special needs children.

Chapter 4 discusses issues of literacy and reading. We walk through my classroom on a typical school day and observe how both requirements and needs can be implemented and accommodated in the classroom.

Chapter 5 introduces us to Karen, a child in remission from brain cancer. By deconstructing data, documents, and work samples, we establish her strengths and demonstrate her growth over time.

Chapter 6 focuses upon creating a literacy program in our classrooms. We look at accommodating various zones of development while incorporating all of the district, state, and federal mandates. Once our curriculum is written we turn to the area of assessment and evaluation. Using various types of data and work samples, we discuss and establish grades.

And because teachers cannot function proactively in isolation, Chapter 7 looks at one way to create a schoolwide literacy program. To support the literacies of our children, teachers and administrators need to come together to establish goals, beliefs, and strategies for implementing literacy programs. These programs need to be based upon sound classroom practice and the way children learn.

Notes

1. One child who was deemed mentally retarded spoke only in occasional grunts. He communicated predominately through print and sign language. He had little muscle control and was incontinent. His favorite time of day was story time and recess.

2. Comprehension was not something I consciously looked for in a good reader at this time.

2

Debbie, Molly, Tony, and the Federal Laws

It is clear that we will see an increase in students with disabilities who are mainstreamed or placed in the classroom on the basis of inclusion. As classroom teachers, we need to know how to advocate for our students and feel comfortable in the special education arena. This means knowing how to identify areas of concern, accommodating students in the regular classroom, and becoming familiar with pertinent laws and procedures. This chapter deals with the law.

Drawing from my own experiences, we travel with three students: Debbie, Molly, and Tony as they each begin their journey into the federal system. All three children are students in my elementary class and my main concern is their academic performance.

Debbie is a student who appears to be of average intelligence, yet is working below her ability and expected grade level. She seems easily confused and frustrated by new academic tasks and appears to require additional time when completing assignments.

Molly is a student described as having above average intelligence and suffers frequently with severe allergies. Her allergy-related absences are numerous and her academics are falling behind. Her allergies hinder her participation in certain school-related activities.

Tony is a student from a low-income household. His family is considered dysfunctional by most school officials. He rarely involves himself in his academic surroundings. When he does produce work, the results suggest that he is a child working below his expected grade level academically and developmentally.

Now What Do I Do?

Recognizing that I need to *do* something is the first step. It's important not to wait for those people I think are responsible or are in charge to inform me of my responsibilities and obligations. As a classroom teacher, I am required by all federal statutes to respond proactively to any indication that a special needs situation may exist.

Identifying the Problem

I begin by trying to formulate the exact nature of my concerns. Why am I worried about Debbie, Molly, and Tony? What am I seeing that bothers me? I clarify my concerns and observations in writing. When documenting, I focus on specific details and examples rather than general impressions or feelings. I supplement my comments with work samples so that I have examples of my observations. Sifting through field notes and work samples, I begin to deconstruct the data and documentation. I look for literacy elements, both strengths and weaknesses, that may provide insight into each of the children's literacy behaviors and language performance.

Reflecting on the Problem

Once I have identified and clarified my concerns, I look at my classroom curriculum and teaching style in relation to each student's problem. I determine how my teaching and curriculum support Debbie, Molly, and Tony in their learning environment. There may be ways that I can adjust my style, negotiate the curriculum, modify our lessons, provide peer grouping, offer more flexibility, or provide other structures and support. I look to see what I can do first.

I make sure that the parents or guardians of Debbie, Molly, and Tony are aware of the situation and my concerns. It's important to contact the parents to discuss (and show) your observations. Parents should never be surprised to find out that their child is having difficulty in school or that there is an academic concern. One of the most important steps you can take to build relationships and avoid conflict is to create and maintain open communication with parents regarding their child's progress.[1]

If there is a chance that the child may be entering the field of special education, then the federal law states that parents must have an opportunity to participate in meetings regarding identification, evaluation, educational services, and educational placement of their child.[2] It is therefore important to document all communication and attempts at communication with all parties involved.

Creating a Student Profile

At this point, I begin to create a student profile for Debbie, Molly, and Tony. Starting with their official cumulative school records, I begin my search for anything that can help me better understand their performance. (See Table 2-1.)

Look In	For	Why
Student Academic Folder	Special Education Folder	Current placement; Previous placement; Previous testing
	Old report cards and school documents	Teacher comments; Prior retentions or academic placements; Working below grade level; attendance and tardies
	Health card	Vision; Hearing; Medical issues
	Work samples	Background information; Analysis

Talk To	Why
Parents	Their impressions; Academic, health, and social history
Previous Teachers	Academic and Social history

Collect	Why
Anecdotal records; Checklists; Work samples; Tests	Analysis; Documentation; Perspective

Table 2-1. Creating a Student Profile

I look for evidence of past or current history in special education. I look to see if they have ever been referred for any special education evaluations or services. If a child has entered the realm of special education for any purpose, then legally there should be a paper trail. These papers should be fairly easy to identify. Typically they are maintained in a separate special education folder inside the child's cumulative record. The documents look official and usually are of various pastel colors, which is typical of carbonless copies used for many school documents. If a special education folder or sign of any special education documents does not exist, then it is logical to assume that there was no official special education involvement in the student's academic past.

To be certain, always check with the school secretary in charge of student records to confirm that all of the child's documentation has been received and is filed in the student's folder. If all records have been received and filed, then be sure to check with the guidance counselors and all special education teachers to see if they might have pulled the special education folder from the child's school record to review for their own purposes.

Next, look at their old report cards. Was Debbie making adequate progress in some areas and poor progress in others? Does it state or note anywhere on Tony's report cards that he was working below grade level? Was he ever retained or administratively placed? What comments have Molly's teachers made in the past? Were Debbie's work habits successful? Did the teacher note or mention that Molly was frequently absent, tardy, or dismissed early? Do any of the teachers express concern or document any type of prior action, such as a child study meeting or request for a conference?

Peruse other record contents for literacy clues. Look for medical data. Most academic folders contain some type of a health record for vision, hearing, and immunizations. Do any records indicate that Debbie has any physical or mental problems? Is Tony taking medication? Does Molly wear glasses?

Look for a portfolio. Many schools are required to maintain specific classroom documents in student portfolios. These usually include writing samples and benchmark tests from a textbook series, such as basal chapter tests and cumulative math tests. Examine these artifacts. What do they show?

In the classroom, I continue to collect work samples and make modifications. I document any and all strategies that I have implemented including the results of those interventions. If anyone assisted me in providing strategies or modifications with Debbie, Molly, or Tony, I document that information also. The documentation helps me to monitor each student's performance and aids me in sharing my observations with all parties concerned. I am able to reflect better upon my teaching and work towards creating a curriculum tailored to each child's needs. My documentation also provides evidence that all federal procedures were followed.

Once my student profiles are complete and I determine that Debbie, Molly, and Tony are in need of services, I must follow the procedures established by my school to schedule a child study meeting.

Child Study

Child study meetings[3] are required by law and are a mandatory first step in the referral process. A child study meeting is any official meeting in which you discuss a student. The meeting is for the purposes of discussing a student's performance, to identify need, and to assist in providing strategies and support. At the child study meeting, I state my specific concerns using my anecdotal records and work samples along with formal assessments. I inform the child study team of any and all interventions, strategies, and/or modifications I have tried along with their respective results. Procedures for child study meetings are required to be in written form. Familiarize yourself with the chain of events and command necessary to readily advocate for each of your students.

All child study meetings are documented and chaired by the student's child study team. Child study teams are determined by federal law and consist of educators who have contact with the student, any people or agencies who are assisting in services, and in some cases, the parents of the child.[4] (See Table 2-2.) Each school creates their own child study team based upon the federal guidelines. In addition to parents and outside providers, team members might include special education teachers, Title 1 teachers, guidance counselors, classroom teachers, special activity teachers, and/or administrators or lead teachers.

The determination of who becomes a team member is decided upon by the type of services you think the child is eligible to receive. This information is discussed in detail later in this chapter. At this stage in your investigation, you need to know that in addition to school personnel, if you believe the child is eligible for any type of special education services, then you must include the child's parents as child study team members from the beginning.

Child Study Meeting #1

Debbie Debbie has no known emotional or physical impairments. She is from an upper-middle class family and is continuously immersed in literacy experiences. Both of her parents are avid readers. Her report cards reflect a

		Checklist
Classroom Teacher	Required	❑
Parent	Required for all special education placements	❑
Special Education Teacher	If Applicable	❑
Physical Therapist	If Applicable	❑
Speech Teacher	Required if the child receives Speech services	❑
Guidance Counselor	Optional	❑
Title 1 Teacher	If Applicable	❑
Administrator	Optional	❑
Individuals with specific knowledge of the child	If Applicable	❑
Representative of a public agency responsible for services or funding	If Applicable	❑

Table 2-2.   Child Study Team Members

child who consistently applies effort, yet continues to produce work below her peers and expectations. She has never been retained or academically placed. She has never been tested for special education services, and her attendance is of no significance to her academics. She does not have a health problem or known impairment, and she is not from a disadvantaged or low-economic home. There may be the possibility that Debbie has a learning disability. Learning disabilities are one area of special education. Members of her child study team, therefore, include her parents and the special education teachers. I contact Debbie's parents personally and then in writing for documentation.

At our first child study meeting we decide that Debbie requires further monitoring. Her demonstrated behaviors are inconsistent with her competencies in other social and academic areas. We brainstorm strategies for supporting Debbie in the classroom. The child study team recommends that Debbie work with a buddy in the areas of reading and math in the classroom. I am to modify her written work allowing her more time and flexibility for the finished products. Her reading materials have already been modified. In addition to her reading-related class work, I will work with Debbie on a one-to-one basis for a minimum of three times per week. Her mother will read with her nightly.

As I begin implementing the strategies established by the child study team, I monitor and document Debbie's performance. At the end of the allotted time (we established six weeks), we will hold a second child study meeting to review Debbie's case. My job is to implement the suggested strategies, continue monitoring Debbie's performance, keep the parents informed, document any meetings and conferences, and assure that Debbie's case and all subsequent actions are handled in a timely fashion and in accordance with the federal statutes (explained later this chapter).

Molly Molly's case is much simpler to identify, yet much harder to accommodate. Molly has allergies that are documented by a physician as limiting her learning. She is unable to benefit from the regular curriculum without modifications. This automatically qualifies Molly for services under Section 504 of the Americans With Disabilities Act (explained later this chapter). Schools are required to have established standards and procedures for the identification, evaluation, and placement of students for Section 504. Lack of established procedures is in itself a violation of the law.

Molly must be assessed as soon as she is suspected of having a disability. I need to refer her for a child study meeting and notify her parent or guardian of my actions. Section 504 differs from the laws pertaining to special education. I do not need to notify Molly's parents in writing, nor do they need to be included as child study team members. I merely need to keep them informed regarding identification, evaluation, and placement. It is up to the individual school districts to determine if the child's parents will be included as child study team members.

Many types of services can be required accommodations under Section 504. It is up to Molly's child study team to decide how best to accommodate Molly's academic and nonacademic needs. The team needs to make sure that the education Molly receives is not limited in any way in comparison to her nondisabled classmates. In Molly's case, there could be a number of solutions and options the team brainstorms and agrees upon. There is no way to predict how Molly's team will provide for her impairment; but legally, the school has to accommodate Molly and pay for expenses incurred. A major difference between Section 504 and special education regulations is that all costs incurred for assessments, services, and modifications are the responsibility of the local educational agency. While Section 504 provides federal protection for the disabled student, it does not provide funds to pay for these accommodations or protection.

In Molly's case we have made provisions to accommodate her absences by providing her with a home school tutor. Frequency of the tutor will be determined by Molly's need. In addition, when allergies flare, Molly's work load will be modified and her class assignments altered so that they may be completed and maintained at home. All allergy-related absences will be legally excused.

I continue to monitor and support Molly in the classroom. I make sure that the modifications established by the child study team under Section 504 are carried out accurately and in a timely manner. I am responsible for Molly's education. It is my job to see that Section 504 helps her. Other than monitoring, Molly's case is closed.

If it appears that final decisions made by Molly's child study team are not adequate for her needs, then my job is to file a complaint of discrimination on Molly's behalf. Any complaints of discrimination are to be filed with the school's compliance officer. A complaint may also be filed with the regional OCR (Office of Civil Rights) either at a later date or simultaneously to notifying the school. Complaints may be filed by any concerned person, educator, or parent, on behalf of the child. Before taking any legal action based upon perceived rights under Section 504, it is suggested that you consult with an attorney for guidance.[5] These issues become highly problematic and uncomfortable. Pursue all options first.

Tony This brings us to Tony. Tony qualifies for free and reduced lunch services at school. Typically this is an indicator that Tony is from a low-income household. His work samples place him at a performance level of approximately two years below his current grade level, and his home situation is considered dysfunctional and at risk by institutional standards. After being tested for a learning disability last year, he did not qualify for special education services. Since I know that he will not be tested again for special education services this year, I recognize that we are not dealing with a special education issue. I notify Tony's parents of my concerns and actions. Because this is not a special education case, the law does not require that they be members of the child study team.

At the child study meeting we determine that Tony's social and academic situation qualifies him for Title 1 services under federal law IASA 94 (explained later this chapter). The amount and type of services and resources that will be provided to Tony will depend upon the school he attends, his need in relation to the other needy students, and the amount of services and resources available. Services under Title 1 are extremely flexible and school specific. Depending on the school, Tony could qualify for a tutor every day—or have no services at all. My job is to accommodate Tony in the classroom and to work closely with support educators to help coordinate and plan his learning.

At our school, Tony will have the support of a Title 1 teacher. She will come into the classroom on a daily basis for forty minutes to work with Tony one-on-one in the area of language arts. Since I am the primary educator responsible for Tony, it is my job is to communicate and coordinate with all those that provide him with academic services. Other than monitoring and supporting Tony in the classroom, Tony's case is closed.

Debbie Enters Special Education

Child Study Meeting # 2

The first child study meeting is for the purposes of recognizing and identifying additional need, support, and strategies. The second child study meeting is required if the child might qualify for special education services as in Debbie's case.

The second child study meeting is for the purpose of reviewing the outcome of the strategies established in the first child study meeting. The team determines if the strategies have been adequate in resolving Debbie's difficulties in the classroom. I inform the team of Debbie's performance over the past six weeks and provide work samples to support my comments. Debbie's parents speak regarding their observations and perceptions. It appears that after six weeks of implementing the suggested strategies we are seeing progress, but not enough to warrant dropping Debbie's case. She requires further support.

The child study team decides to evaluate Debbie for a possible learning disability. Debbie will be tested by trained professionals[6] in accordance with the federal guidelines. When her testing has been completed and scored, we will hold a third child study meeting for the purpose of reviewing these tests.

Child Study Meeting # 3

At this meeting, all testing on Debbie has been completed and scored. We are meeting for the purpose of reviewing the test data. This is considered an eligibility meeting. We will try to determine:

- if more data is needed
- if Debbie has a particular category of disability
- if the testing establishes that Debbie is eligible for special education services
- Debbie's present level of tested performance
- if Debbie will benefit from special education services

If Debbie's test scores confirm that she's eligible for special education services, and it is decided that she will benefit from these services, then the next step is to review all data to create and formalize her individual educational program (IEP).

Debbie's individual educational program (IEP) outlines the details of her educational plan for the academic school year. It includes such items as a statement of all special education services she will receive, a list of any supplemental aids or services that will be provided for Debbie, and it establishes modifications that I am required to make in the classroom and in her other curricular activities.

All special education laws regarding IEPs are contained in the federal document known as the Individuals With Disabilities Education Act, commonly referred to as IDEA 97. The requirements regarding IEPs are located in Appendix C of IDEA 97. These regulations were effective as of July 1, 1998.[7]

Debbie's IEP

IEP Requirements There are specific academic components that must be written into all IEPs to remain in compliance with the law. Table 2-3 summarizes these requirements. Debbie's IEP must include:

- A statement of her present level of academic performance.[8] This contains information as to how Debbie's disability affects her involvement in the regular curriculum.
- A statement of her measurable annual goals including benchmarks or short-term objectives.[9] Appendix C goes on to state that once we, the IEP team, have developed measurable annual goals for Debbie, we can then utilize these goals to help refine effective strategies to achieve the goals consistent with Debbie's needs. We can also use the goals to develop short-term objectives and benchmarks that will enable Debbie's family,

The IEP Includes	The IEP Includes (cont.)
Present level of academic performance	The IEP was written within 30 days of determination
A statement of measurable annual goals	The IEP was not completed prior to the IEP meeting
A statement of benchmarks and short-term objectives	"All members of the child study team, including parents, had input"
A statement detailing all special education and related services	*Monitoring the IEP*
A statement of testing modifications if applicable	The IEP was in effect before any services were provided
An explanation of the extent to which the child will not participate in the regular classroom and/or activities	The IEP is monitored and reviewed periodically; but at least every 12 months
Transition services to work and post-school experiences (if applicable)	The IEP was completed and in place at the beginning of the school year
Representative of a public agency responsible for services or funding	The parents have a copy and understand all services provided

Table 2-3. IEP Requirements

Debbie, and her teachers to monitor her progress and program throughout the year.

- A statement that details all special education and related services Debbie will receive, and that lists the supplementary aids and services that will be provided for her or on her behalf.[10]

A statement must also be included establishing the program modifications that will be provided for Debbie, as well as the support that will be provided for the school personnel that work with Debbie. This provision is to ensure that Debbie appropriately advances toward her established goals, that she be involved in the general curriculum, and that she participate in extracurricular and nonacademic activities. It also establishes that she can be educated and participate with other children with and/or without disabilities in nonacademic situations.

- An explanation of the extent, if any, to which Debbie will not participate with nondisabled children in the regular classroom and in extracurricular nonacademic activities.[11]
- A statement of any individual modifications in the administration of state or district-wide assessments of student achievement that are needed for Debbie to participate in the assessment.[12] If the IEP team determines that Debbie will not participate in the assessment of student achievement, then a statement explaining why that assessment is not appropriate for Debbie and how Debbie will be assessed is needed.[13]

Regulations Regarding Child Study Team Members Regulations are very clear regarding the members of the child study team for Debbie.

- If Debbie is involved in regular education in any manner, then at least one of Debbie's regular education teachers must be a member of the child study team.[14]
- Debbie's parent or guardian must be a member of the team.[15]

Writing The IEP

Once eligibility has been determined, the team writes Debbie's IEP for the school year. We have the option of writing Debbie's IEP while we are at the third child study meeting, or convening and holding another meeting for the purpose of writing Debbie's IEP. In regard to modifications and services for her IEP, we need to consider all information and perspectives brought to the table. This includes parental suggestions and input, special education suggestions and input, my suggestions and input, Debbie's student profile, class samples, and the results of Debbie's testing.

It is required that Debbie remain in the least restrictive environment that supports her needs. In considering modifications, we want to accommodate Debbie with as little disruption in her regular classroom routine as possible. Modifications could include:

- additional time allowances on class work and tests
- taking standardized tests in an individual one-on-one setting rather than a group setting
- adjusting curriculum and materials to suit Debbie's performance, learning style, strengths, and developmental level
- providing classroom support through a resource teacher that works with Debbie in the classroom
- providing classroom support through a resource teacher that works with Debbie outside the classroom
- peer tutors

After the IEP Is Written and Agreed Upon

Once Debbie's IEP is written, understood, and agreed upon by all team members, it is my responsibility to implement the specific details and elements into our classroom setting.

Debbie's special education teacher will support me in the classroom and work with Debbie to the extent that her IEP specifies. Debbie will remain in the regular classroom for most of the day and I will be the primary educator responsible for her instruction and delivery of instruction. She will work with the special education teacher on a pull-out basis three days a week for forty minutes in the area of reading.

When it comes time for interim progress reports and quarterly report cards, her special education teacher and I will negotiate Debbie's grade. Her special education teacher will attend to all needed documents, timelines, reviews, evaluations, and meetings necessary to remain in compliance with the federal guidelines for learning disabilities and IEPs. Debbie's progress will continue to be monitored. Her IEP will be monitored daily and updated yearly unless there is reason to update her IEP sooner. Debbie's case is considered closed.

Federal Programs

In order to advocate for our students, there are three federal laws that we need to know (see Table 2-4 for summary and procedures). These laws

Procedure	Special Education (IDEA 97)	Title 1 (IASA 94)	Medical (Section 504)
Identify concerns	X	X	X
Create a student profile	X	X	X
Notify parents	X	X	X
Schedule child study team meeting	X	X	X
Child study meeting #1	X	X	X
Implement and document strategies	X	X	X
Child study meeting #2	X		
Testing	X		
Child study meeting #3	X		
IEP	X		
Implement services	X	X	X
Document, monitor, collaborate, accommodate	X	X	X

Table 2-4. Federal Program Procedures

are: The Individuals with Disabilities Act (referred to as IDEA 97), which governs all of special education; Section 504 of the Rehabilitation Act (referred to as Section 504), which is a civil rights act that protects the constitutional rights of all persons of disability; and The Improving American School's Act 1994 (referred to as IASA 94), which oversees such programs as Title 1. Refer to Table 2-5 for more information concerning these statutes.

Debbie has qualified for special education due to a learning disability. To support Debbie, I followed all federal guidelines under IDEA 97. Molly has medical issues and is protected by Section 504. Tony is considered at risk by federal definition. His academic program and services need to adhere to IASA 94 standards. Knowing each law and what it covers is a major step in advocating and providing services for your students.

IDEA 97	Section 504	IASA 94
Specific learning disabilities	Diabetes	Limited English Proficiency (LEP)
Mental retardation	Allergies or Asthma	Migratory students
Hearing impairments	Communicable diseases	Homeless students
Deafness	Temporary disabilities	Students deemed at risk
Speech or language impairments	Environmental illnesses	Preschool children
Visual impairments	Drug or alcohol addiction	
Blindness	Numerous medical issues: if in doubt—Check!	
Serious emotional disturbance		
Orthopedic impairments		
Autism		
Traumatic brain injury		

Table 2-5. Federal Statutes

The Individuals with Disabilities Education Act: IDEA 97

What Is It? Federal law regarding special education became mandatory in 1975 with the passage of The Education for All Handicapped Children Act (Public Law 94–142).[16] After being amended and renamed numerous times, IDEA 97 is the latest Individuals With Disabilities Education Act to which schools must comply. The new statute can be located in the United States Code (U.S.C.), Volume 20, beginning at section 1400 (20 U.S.C.§1400). The Federal Register is also published on the Internet and provides access to the most recent information regarding laws, acts, and regulations.[17]

Important new provisions have been added in the areas of performance goals and indicators, the IEP, the IEP team, parents participation in placement, support programs, and legal fees. These are highlighted in the following sections.

Special Education Regulations

Child Study Team

- It is required that the child study team include at least one regular education teacher of the child if that child is participating in a regular classroom environment.[18]

- Parents must have an opportunity to participate in meetings regarding identification, evaluation, educational program, and educational placement of the child.[19]

- Parents must be part of the teams that determine what additional data is needed as part of an evaluation, as eligibility criteria, and for placement of their child.[20]

- The IEP team must include a representative of those qualified to provide and supervise specially designed instruction to meet the needs of children with disabilities, have knowledge of the general curriculum, and be knowledgeable about the availability of services.[21] In most schools, this role is usually filled by the special education teacher who will be providing or recommending the services.

- A speech-language pathologist must be included on the IEP team if the child's disability is speech related. If the child's disability is predominately speech related then the speech-language pathologist may be the special education representative at the IEP meeting. However, speech must be considered special education under state standards, and a regular classroom teacher must still be in attendance if the child participates in a regular classroom setting.

- If a child receives related services, a representative of that service need only attend those meetings in which the service is being discussed.

Determining Eligibility If it is determined that the child requires further screening, all federal procedures and timelines regarding eligibility, IEPs and services, and monitoring progress must be followed.

- Once parental consent is secured for an initial evaluation to determine if services are required for a student, the school must ensure that the evaluation is accomplished within a *reasonable period of time.*[22]

- A meeting in which a determination is made that a student requires services may be continued to develop the IEP and establish placement of that student.[23]

Writing the IEP

- Once a determination is made that the student requires services, the IEP must be developed within 30 calendar days and implemented as soon as possible following the meeting in which the IEP is developed.[24]
- In notifying parents about the IEP meeting, the school must indicate the purpose, time, location, and who will be in attendance.[25]
- The school should inform the parents of their right to invite to the meeting other individuals who have knowledge or special expertise regarding the child. It is also appropriate for the public agency to inquire of the parents if they will be inviting other individuals to the meeting.[26]
- The public agency shall invite to the IEP meeting a representative of any other public agency that may be responsible for providing or paying for transition services. To meet this statute, the school must establish and implement procedures that would ensure the identification of all agencies likely to have responsibility for these services, and invite them to the IEP meeting.[27]
- The IEP team, at the discretion of the parents or public agency, may invite other individuals who have *specific knowledge* or expertise regarding the child.[28] This is a change from the prior law that allowed, without qualification, *any* individual to attend IEP meetings at the discretion of the parent or school. Part B does not provide for participation of individuals, such as lawyers or representatives of teacher organizations, at IEP meetings. Such individuals may only be in attendance if they have specific knowledge regarding the child, not just the situation; the presence of these individuals must not create an adversarial climate.
- Parents must have their concerns and information considered in developing and reviewing their child's IEPs.[29]
- An IEP must be in effect before special education and related services are provided to a child.[30]
- An IEP must not be completed before the IEP meeting begins. School personnel may come to the IEP meeting prepared with the evaluations and recommendations, but they must make clear to the parents at the outset of the meeting that the services proposed by the agency are only recommendations to review and discuss.

- The amount of services to be received must be stated on the IEP in such a manner that the parents and IEP team members clearly understand the specifics of what is being provided. The amount of time committed to each service must also be noted, and the time allotted must be appropriate to the service being implemented.
- Parents have a right to a copy of their child's IEP.[31]

Monitoring Progress
- Schools must initiate and conduct IEP meetings periodically, but at least every twelve months. An IEP must be in place for all students at the beginning of the school year and the components must reflect services that can be implemented adequately. Although it is the school's responsibility for determining time frames of IEPs, the parents of a child with a disability have a right to request an IEP at any time. If a child's teacher feels that the child's placement or IEP services are not appropriate, the teacher should follow the school's procedures regarding calling or meeting with parents, or request that the team hold another IEP meeting.[32]
- Parents must be regularly informed by such means as report cards at least as often as nondisabled students. They need to be notified regarding the child's progress, the child's progress in meeting the IEP goals, and the extent to which that progress is sufficient to enable the child to achieve their established goals by the end of the year.[33]
- The public agency must ensure that the child's IEP is complied to as written. To assure this, the public agency may use whatever state, local, federal, and private sources of support that are available for those purposes.[34] The services must be at no cost to the parent and the public agency must remain responsible for compliance with the IEP.

Student Transfers If a child with a disability changes school districts in the same state, the new school site is responsible for ensuring that the child receive established services. The new school must ensure that the student has an IEP in effect before they provide any services. The IEP may be transferred from the previous school site under the following conditions:

- a copy of the current IEP is available
- the parents indicate they are satisfied with the current IEP
- the new school site determines that the current IEP is appropriate and can be implemented as written

Recorded Devices Part B does not address the use of audio or video recording devices at IEP meetings. There are also no federal statutes that either authorize or prohibit the recording of an IEP meeting. Therefore, the SEA (State Educational Agency) or public agency (such as the school) has the option to require, prohibit, limit, and/or regulate the use of recording devices at IEP meetings. If the public agency has a policy regarding recording devices at IEP meetings, then that agency must provide exceptions (if needed) to ensure that the parents understand the IEP and IEP process, or to make sure that the parents' rights are being implemented as guaranteed under Part B. Any recording of an IEP meeting made by a public agency becomes an official document (an education record) and would be subject to confidentiality requirements. Parents wishing to record IEP meetings should consult state or local policies for further guidance.

Section 504

Section 504 of the Rehabilitation Act applies to persons with disabilities. It is a civil rights act that protects the civil and constitutional rights of disabled persons by prohibiting organizations that receive federal funds from discriminating against otherwise qualified individuals based solely upon their disability. Section 504 is enforced by the U.S. Department of Education, Office of Civil Rights (OCR).

Section 504 and IDEA 97: What's the Difference? While we hear frequently about responsibilities related to federal law IDEA 97, schools are less proactive in their identification and enforcement of Civil Right's Act Section 504.

- Section 504 is proactive. It is intended to create an equal playing field among all individuals by dissolving barriers that exclude persons with disabilities. Requesting a handicap ramp in front of a grocery store or excluding a child from a classroom because they have cancer would fall under Section 504.

  IDEA 97 is remedial. It establishes that in addition to creating the level playing field secured in Section 504, persons with disabilities are also entitled to receive certain services and programs from the public agency responsible for services to the child.

- Section 504 requires that schools do not discriminate. However, it does not provide any additional funding to help the schools comply. Therefore, a school site becomes responsible for any and all expenses incurred that were necessary under Section 504. While IDEA 97 requires that schools provide more services to children with disabilities, it also provides the school with additional funding to help facilitate their compliance.

• Section 504 applies to education agencies that receive any amount of federal funding. IDEA 97 applies to schools that are seeking to obtain federal funding.

• Section 504 contains a broad definition of what is considered a disability. Because of this, all children covered under IDEA 97 are also covered by Section 504; but not all children covered by Section 504 are covered by IDEA 97. This means that not all children with disabilities are covered under IDEA 97. Only those children who meet the eligibility criteria based upon IDEA's definition of a handicap or disability are allowed services under IDEA. Section 504 protects all persons with a disability. Their definition of a disability is much broader than IDEA's and includes all persons who have a mental or physical impairment that substantially limits one or more major life activities. The person must also have a record of their impairment or at least be regarded as having such impairment.

Section 504 defines a person with a physical or mental impairment as any physiological disorder or condition, cosmetic disfiguration, or anatomical loss. Physical impairments must affect one or more of the following body systems: neurological, digestive, skin or endocrine, respiratory (including speech organs), cardiovascular, reproductive, hemic and lymphatic, special sense organs, and/or musculoskeletal. Mental or psychological disorders include mental retardation, organic brain syndrome, emotional or mental illness, and specific learning disabilities. The impairment must have a substantial affect on one or more major life activities. A major life activity according to Section 504 includes caring for oneself, walking, seeing, hearing, speaking, breathing, learning, working, and/or performing manual tasks. The critical question for schools is whether the student's impairment substantially limits[35] their ability to learn. It is not true that the impairment must be of a life activity other than or in addition to learning.

• IDEA defines FAPE (Free Appropriate Public Education) as including the provision of special education and related services. Section 504's definition of FAPE includes regular or special education and related services.

• IDEA focuses upon the individual educational needs of the impaired student. Section 504 looks at comparing the education and services of students with and without disabilities.

- School districts must establish separate written procedures for Section 504. Districts that evaluate only those students who fall within IDEA categories are not in compliance with the law. Schools should emphasize that a student may require an evaluation under Section 504 even if there is no reason to suspect that the student is in need of special education services under an IEP. Similar to IDEA, Section 504 has specific procedural requirements for the identification, evaluation, placement, and procedural safeguards of preschool, elementary, and secondary students.
- There are no specific timelines for implementing Section 504. As with IDEA, the regulations are required to be adhered to within a reasonable time.
- Placement regulations under Section 504 are comparable to IDEA, however, Section 504 does not prescribe the membership team. It is up to the district to determine if parents will be included as members of the team.
- Least Restrictive Environment (LRE) definitions remain the same between Section 504 and IDEA.
- With regard to LRE, under Section 504 a student that is expelled or suspended from school for more than ten consecutive days is considered to have a *significant change of placement*. In addition, before a student protected under Section 504 is suspended for more than ten days cumulatively in a school year, the placement team needs to determine whether the series of suspensions creates a pattern that could be considered a significant change in placement.
- Section 504 requires notification of parents regarding identification, evaluation, and placement of a student; but unlike IDEA, this notification does not have to be in writing.
- There is no consent requirement needed under Section 504. IDEA requires written parental consent prior to initial evaluations and placement of their child.
- Section 504 requires a plan describing placement and services. IDEA requires an IEP.
- School districts must designate an employee to be responsible for assuring Section 504 compliance and must provide a grievance procedure.

Section 504 Compliance and Grievance Procedures A student or a parent has a right to file a complaint if there is suspected discrimination. The complaint should be filed initially with the school or school district's compliance officer.

If a school or school district does not have a compliance officer, then that in itself is a violation. Filing a complaint with the school does not limit access to other enforcement options. Section 504 (unlike IDEA) does not have a state agency in place to assure that schools are complying with their responsibilities.

The Office for Civil Rights (usually the regional office) conducts compliance reviews and complaint investigations in addition to technical assistance activities. Complaints may be filed through the Office for Civil Rights by an individual or organization, and the complaint may address individual student, class, or systemic issues. Although the complaint is required to be filed within 180 days of the alleged discriminatory action, the Regional Director has the authority to waive the time limit.

The OCR will investigate the allegation through data collection, written responses, and on-site visits. OCR will then issue a Letter of Findings, which will identify the violations or conclude that no violation exists. Failure to implement the corrective actions requested by OCR could lead to an administrative hearing resulting in the loss of federal funds. When determining compliance, OCR looks to see if the school district has followed the policy and procedural requirements under the law. It does not concern itself with second-guessing the educational decisions made by the school—only that the school followed the correct procedures regarding the identification, placement, and evaluation of the student.

Eligibility A student or parent may initiate a court action alleging discrimination under Section 504. There are now grounds for awarding monetary damages as well as the possibility of recovering personal damage from public agencies. The court also has the discretion to authorize that attorney fees be awarded to the prevailing party. Section 504 is easily overlooked as a support option in many school systems. I have been teaching for ten years, and prior to this research, never heard of Section 504. That in itself is breaking the law.

The following are examples of students who may be protected under Section 504, but not IDEA:

- students with diabetes
- students with allergies or asthma
- students with communicable diseases (for example, hepatitis)
- students with temporary disabilities arising from accidents who may need short-term hospitalization or homebound recovery
- students with environmental illnesses
- students who are drug or alcohol addicted, as long as they are not currently using illegal drugs

In schools, a student could be considered the victim of discrimination in some of the following situations:

- refusing to allow a student with an IEP the opportunity to be on the honor roll
- denying credit to a student whose absenteeism is related to the disability
- refusing to dispense medication to a student with ADHD
- determining sports eligibility based upon a student's grades without consideration of the disability
- placing a student with a hearing impairment in the front row instead of providing an interpreter[36]
- sponsoring a student organization that excludes persons with disabilities
- denying a student a place on a planning board or committee because of the impairment
- limiting the enjoyment of any right, privilege, advantage, or opportunity enjoyed by others
- locating students with disabilities in inferior facilities due to lack of classroom space

The Improving American School's Act 1994 (IASA)[37]

IASA 94 provides resources to states, districts, and schools to support their efforts to help students reach high state standards. It replaces the Elementary and Secondary Education Act of 1965 (ESEA). IASA programs include:

- Helping Disadvantaged Students Meet High Standards (Title I, Part A)
- The Education of Migratory Children (Title 1, Part C)
- The Eisenhower Professional Development Program (Title II)[38]
- The Safe and Drug-Free Schools and Communities Act of 1994 (Title IV)
- The Bilingual Education Act (Title VII)
- The Indian Education Program (Title IX)
- The Public Charter Schools Program (Title X)
- The Coordinated Services Program (Title XI)

IASA 94 pertains to programs that support students who are considered to be disadvantaged or at risk in our public school system. Whereas, IDEA 97 and Section 504 pertain to protecting individual children who have special needs, IASA 94 pertains to programs that were established to proactively help disadvantaged children meet the same high academic standards expected of all public school children. This legislation includes bilingual education programs, programs for children deemed economically deprived (Title 1), safe and drug-free school programs, and/or programs for staff development.

IASA also contains its own set of federal guidelines and eligibility criteria that needs to be adhered to in the school system. Similar to Section 504, identification and recommendation for student services under IASA will most likely be initiated by the classroom teacher. IASA is usually heavily supported and adhered to within the schools. Federal funding is contingent upon following the criteria of IASA so most schools tend to assure compliance.

Eligibility Title 1 targets children in school attendance areas of high poverty relative to their school district. Students may participate in Title 1 programs if they are attending a school that receives Title 1 targeted assistance or maintains a schoolwide Title 1 program. Children at a targeted assistance school must be identified based upon eligibility criteria established at each individual school site. Schoolwide programs are not required to identify particular children for participation. LEP (Limited English Proficiency) students, migratory students, homeless students, students deemed at risk, and preschool children can be served by Title 1.

As stated earlier with Tony, compliance with IASA is dependent upon the status of your school. If you are not at a Title 1 school, then there are not IASA services available at your school and no compliance is available or necessary. If you are at a Title 1 school, your responsibilities vary depending upon whether your school is implementing a schoolwide program or it receives targeted assistance.

If you are teaching at a school implementing a schoolwide Title 1 program, then all of your students are eligible to utilize Title 1 materials and resources. It will be your responsibility as the classroom teacher to assist the Title 1 staff in identifying those children in your class who would best benefit from Title 1 instruction. Title 1 teachers are required to prioritize student services based upon demonstrated need. Your individual school site will establish the criteria you need to identify children in your class who could best benefit from direct instruction through Title 1 services.

The school site is responsible for designing their schoolwide Title 1 program in accordance with federal guidelines. Title 1 programs become official federal programs, and services vary from school to school depending upon the priorities and needs of each school population.

If you are teaching at a school with Targeted Assistance, then your classroom students will need to be identified as being Title 1 students before they are permitted to utilize Title 1 materials or services. However, it is perfectly legal to utilize Title 1 materials with children who are not classified as Title 1 if you can show or determine how this use benefits your Title 1 child. Let's say that Tony is my only Title 1 student. Rather than have Tony work by himself, it has been considered important that Tony receive experience in small group discussions and projects. Therefore, when his Title 1 teacher[39] enters the room to work with Tony, it is now legal for the Title 1 teacher to work with non-Title 1 students in Tony's group because their involvement aids in supporting Tony.

Title 1 teachers are required to maintain all necessary legal documents and assessment criteria. As a classroom teacher, my main responsibilities are to help identify need and support Tony in the classroom. Title 1 does not necessitate a written individualized education plan for each child; however, documenting progress and the effectiveness of Title 1 programs is becoming a prominent issue. Accountability is becoming more stringent from the federal level down to the individual schools. I can only presume that some of this accountability in the form of paperwork may eventually filter down from the Title 1 teacher to the classroom teacher. However, because schools' Title 1 programs are capable of being rewritten and formatted yearly, it is the schools' responsibility to keep their staff updated concerning their Title 1 program and procedures. If you are a teacher at a Title 1 school and do not know your school's procedures, then it is your obligation to find out.

Knowing the federal laws and procedures is the first step toward advocating for our students. I am now in a better position to consider all options and possibilities. In order to accommodate the law and my children, I must continue my investigation by looking at the issues that surround mainstreaming, inclusion, and federal support programs. These issues will be addressed in Chapter 3.

Chapter 2 Appendix

Terminology

To better understand the services available, it is important to know the operational definitions used in the federal statutes. The laws and regulations are intentionally worded very specifically. If a situation or case ever has to go to due process,[40] all documents involved need to be accurate and compliant with the law—including the language.

To protect your student, make sure that you are aware of the specific legal definitions employed by each federal document. An error in interpretation could be considered against the law in this arena. In the court system, there is a difference between what is morally right and what is legally binding; there is no such thing as *good intentions*. The following is a list of terms and/or phrases along with their operational definitions that are used in pertinent federal documents. Because there are differences in definitions between the various terms in the three main documents, each document is handled separately.

IDEA 97

The following terms are from IDEA 97 and defined in Section 1401 of the Act.

Assistive technology device: Any item, piece of equipment, or product system that is used to maintain, increase, or improve functional capabilities of a child with a disability. These devices may be acquired commercially off the shelf, modified, or customized.

Assistive technology service: Any service that directly assists a child with a disability in the selection, acquisition, or use of an assistive technology device. This includes the evaluation of the needs of the child, providing for the acquisition of the assistive technology device, selecting, fitting, repairing and maintaining the assistive technology device, coordinating and using other therapists and services with assistive technology devices, training and technical assistance for the child and the family as well as professionals, such as educators and employers, who are involved in the life of the child.

Child with a disability: In general, a child with mental retardation, hearing impairments, deafness, speech or language impairments, visual impairments, blindness, serious emotional disturbance, orthopedic impairments, autism, traumatic brain injury, other health impairments, or specific learning disabilities, who by reason thereof requires special education services.

Children ages 3–9 may, at the discretion of the state and local educational agency, include a child who is experiencing developmental delays as defined by the state and measured by the appropriate diagnostic instruments and procedures. The developmental delay may be in one or more of the following areas: physical development, cognitive development, communication development, social or emotional development, or adaptive development.

Educational service agency: A regional multiservice agency that is authorized by state law to develop, manage, and provide services or programs to local agencies. This agency is recognized as an administrative agency for purposes of the provision of special education and related services provided within public elementary and secondary schools. The term also includes any other public institution or agency that has administrative control and direction over a public school.

Equipment: Equipment includes machinery, utilities, built-in equipment, and any necessary enclosures or structures to house the machinery, utilities, or equipment. All items necessary for the functioning of a facility for the provision of educational services (such as an elementary school) are also included. These items could include furniture, printed materials, audiovisual instructional materials, technological aids and devices, books, periodicals, documents, and other related materials.

Excess cost: Any expenses that are in excess of the average annual per student expenditure in the local educational agency during the preceding school year for an elementary or secondary student.

Free Appropriate Public Education (FAPE): Special education and related services that have been provided at public expense under public supervision and direction without charge. These services must meet the standards of the State Educational Agency and include preschool, elementary, or secondary education. Services need also be provided in conformity with the individualized education program required under section 1414(d).

Indian: Any individual who is a member of an Indian tribe.

Indian tribe: Any federal or state Indian tribe, band, ranchero, pueblo, colony, or community including any Alaskan native village or regional village corporation (as defined in or established under the Alaska Native Claims Settlement Act).

Individualized education program (IEP): A written statement for each child with a disability that is developed, reviewed, and revised in accordance with section 1414(d).

Local educational agency: A public board of education or other public authority legally constituted within a state for either administrative control or direction of a public school, or to perform a service function for a public school. (The definition goes on to add that the services are for public schools in a city, county, township, school district, or other political subdivision of a state.)

This term also includes an elementary or secondary school funded by the Bureau of Indian Affairs, but only to the extent that such inclusion makes the school eligible for programs that are not already provided under provision of law.

Native language: Uscd with reference to an individual of limited English proficiency; the language normally used by the individual. In the case of a child (*child* not defined), this would be the language normally used by the parents of the child.

Parent: Includes a legal guardian, and except as used in sections 1415(b)(2) and 1439(a)(5), includes an individual assigned under one of those sections to be a surrogate parent.

Related services: Transportation, developmental, corrective, and other supportive services as required to assist the child with a disability or to benefit from special education. This includes the early identification and assessment of disabling conditions in children as well as speech-language pathology, therapeutic recreation, social work services, counseling services, rehabilitation counseling, and medical services that are for diagnostic and evaluation purposes only.

Secondary school: A nonprofit school that provides secondary education as determined by state law. This does not include education beyond grade twelve.

Special education: Specially designed instruction at no cost to parents that meets the unique needs of a child with a disability. This includes instruction in the classroom, home, or hospital and institution settings; also instruction in physical education.

Specific learning disability: A disorder in one or more of the basic psychological processes involved in understanding or in using spoken or written language. The disorder may manifest itself as an inability to listen, think, speak, read, write, spell, or perform mathematical calculations. Disorders include perceptual disabilities, brain injury, minimal brain dysfunction, dyslexia, and developmental aphasia. Disorders do not include a learning problem that is primarily the result of visual, hearing, or motor disabilities. It does not include mental retardation, emotional disturbance, or environmental, cultural, or economic disadvantage.

State educational agency: The state board of education or other agency or officer primarily responsible for the state supervision of public schools. If no such officer or agency exists, then one is designated by the governor or by state law.

Supplemental aids and services: Aids, services, and related support that are provided in regular education classes or other education-related settings that allow children with disabilities to be educated with nondisabled children to the maximum extent appropriate in accordance with section 1412(a)(5).

Transition services: A coordinated set of activities for a student with a disability that promotes movement from school to post-school activities. This includes post-secondary education, vocational training, integrated employment, continuing and adult education, adult services, independent living, or community participation. These services are based upon the individual's needs and take into account the student's preferences and interests. Services may include instruction, community experiences, the development of employment, or acquisition of daily living skills.

Section 504

Disability: A person who has a physical or mental impairment that limits one or more major life activities. This impairment must be documented or the person must be regarded as having such an impairment.

FAPE (Free Appropriate Public Education): An education provided by the public school system, which includes regular or special education and their related services and aids. This education must be designed to accommodate the individual needs of persons with disabilities as adequately as the needs of nondisabled students.

LRE (Least Restrictive Environment): LRE is defined consistently in all three documents. It is the federal government's presumption that disabled students will be educated alongside their peers in the regular classroom setting unless otherwise documented as to why this placement is not in the best interest of the disabled student. (This is where the concept of inclusion comes from.)

Major life activity: Includes such activities as walking, seeing, hearing, speaking, learning, working, caring for oneself, and performing manual tasks. It is not true that the impairment be of a life activity other than or in addition to learning.

Substantially limits: (as used in the phrase, *substantially limits the ability to learn*) There is no measure by which to quantify this phrase. However, when determining discrimination, both academic and nonacademic activities need to be considered. If a child cannot participate in any school related activity because of their impairment then the student's learning has become *limited*.

IASA 94: Title 1

Adequate yearly progress: The measure set by each state to evaluate the performance of Title 1 schools and districts. This definition varies from state to state. The intent is to see continuous substantial yearly improvement among the children served under Title 1.

At risk: School aged youth who are at risk of academic failure, have drug or alcohol problems, are pregnant or are parents, have come into contact with the juvenile justice system, are gang members, are at least one year behind expected grade level, have high absenteeism rates, or have dropped out of school at one time or another.

Continuous improvement: Refers to self-regulating systems that use internal or external measures to monitor progress toward some end result or goal.

Eligible school attendance area: A school attendance area where the percentage of children from low-income families is at least as high as the percentage of children from low-income families in the local education agency as a whole.

Performance assessment: When students create a product or undertake an action that demonstrates their knowledge or skills. This assessment requires that the student produce an answer rather than simply select one from an array of choices.

Performance indicators: A performance measure (such as benchmarks) that shows the degree to which a student is meeting their desired goals and objectives.

Performance standards: Concrete examples of what students need to know and be able to do to demonstrate proficiency in each content area.

Pull-out model of instruction: Method of instruction in which students are removed from their regular classroom setting, usually for small group instruction.

Schoolwide programs: Title 1 schools with at least 50 percent poverty may qualify for schoolwide programs. These schools may combine Part A funds with other federal, state, and/or local funds to serve all children and upgrade the entire educational program.

Targeted assistance programs: Title 1 schools that are not eligible or choose not to conduct schoolwide programs. These schools serve only those students from low-income families who are identified by the school as failing or at risk of failing.

Notes

1. Resources for this section primarily obtained from
    a. Hallahan, Daniel P. and James M. Kauffman. 1991. *Exceptional Children Introduction to Special Education.* Boston: Allyn and Bacon.
    b. Federal documents: IDEA 97, Section 504 of the Americans With Disabilities Act and IASA.
2. Sections 300.344(a)(1) and 300.517 of IDEA 97.
3. The term *child study* is not an official term used by the federal government. Your school may simply refer to these meetings as calling a parent conference.
4. Parents must be included in all child study team meetings. Section 1414(b)(4) now requires that determination of eligibility for services will be decided by a team that includes the parents.
5. Rosenfeld, S. James. 1997. "Section 504 and IDEA: Basic Similarities and Differences." Available at http://www.edlaw.net or www.ldonline.org/ld
6. Usually the special education teacher or guidance counselor.
7. Appendix C to Part 300—Notice of Interpretation Authority: Individuals with Disabilities Education Act (20 U.S.C. 1401, et seq.).

8. Section 300.347(a)(1).

9. Section 300.347(a)(2).

10. Section 300.347(a)(3).

11. Section 300.347(a)(4). This is consistent with the provisions established in Sections 300.553 regarding Least Restrictive Environment.

12. Section 300.347(a)(5).

13. Section 300.347(a)(5).

14. Section 300.344(a)(2).

15. Section 1414 (b)(4).

16. Hallahan, Daniel P. and James M. Kauffman. 1991. *Exceptional Children Introduction to Special Education.* Boston: Allyn and Bacon.

17. The following Web sites should prove helpful:

    U.S. Department of Education: http: //www.ed.gov/offices/OSERS/IDEA
    LD Online: http://www.ldonline.org
    Special Education Advocate: http://www.wrightslaw.com

18. Section 300.344(a)(2).

19. Sections 300.344(a)(1) and 300.517.

20. Sections 300.533(a)(1); 300.534(a)(1); and 300. 501(c).

21. Section 300.344(a)(4).

22. Section 300.343(b).

23. Section 300.534(a)(1). All provisions of Part B (requirements for IEP meetings) and the requirements affecting eligibility decisions as stated in Section 300.533 must be adhered to.

24. Section 300.343(b)(2).

25. Section 300.345(b).

26. Section 300.344(a)(6).

27. Section. 300.347(b)(1)(ii).

28. Section 300.344(a)(6).

29. Sections 300.343(c)(iii) and 300.346(a)(1)(i) and (b).

30. Section 300.342(b)(1).

31. Section 300.345(f).

32. Sections 300.343(c) and 300.342(a).

33. Section 300.347(a)(7).

34. Section 300.301(a).

35. The term *substantially limits* is not defined, and there is no qualifiable standard by which it can be applied. To determine if a student's learning is substantially limited the schools must consider academic and nonacademic activities. If a child with allergies is barred from a field trip because of the impairment, then the student's learning is *limited*.

36. The student with the impairment must be afforded the provisions of aids, services, and benefits that are equally effective as those provided to others. *Equally effective* is not defined as *identical*. It means *equivalent* and the student must be provided with an equal opportunity, not equal results.

37. All information from this section is from the U.S. Department of Education, Richard Riley, Secretary, U.S. Department of Education. (1995). "The improving America's School Act of 1994 Reauthorization of the Elementary and Secondary Act." This information can be located at http://www.ed.gov/legislation/ESEA.

38. The Eisenhower Professional Development program (Title II) supports sustained, intensive, high-quality professional development tied to achieving the state academic standards. These standards are required of all students including Title I, Title VII, and Title IX children. Title II funds are tied directly to professional development efforts that assist school districts and schools to meet the needs of their students. States and school districts may choose to consolidate their federal administrative funds and administer those funds in a coordinated way without having to keep detailed records. The law also allows states and local districts to consolidate their plans and applications when they apply for federal funding.

39. The Title 1 teacher (or teachers) at a school are hired to work specifically with Title 1 students. The Title 1 teacher is typically not the same instructor as the special education resource person or speech pathologist. The term *Title 1 teacher* does not refer to a regular classroom teacher who is implementing and/or accommodating Title 1 strategies in the classroom.

40. States must provide parents an opportunity for a due process hearing to resolve complaints. In filing a complaint, parents are required to include in their request for a hearing a notice that includes the name and address of the child, the school the child is attending, a description of the nature of the problem, and the facts relating to the problem. Each state is required to establish a voluntary mediation process. The parents have the right to recover reasonable attorneys' fees and costs if they prevail in administrative or judicial proceedings under IDEA.

3

Applying the Federal Laws in Your Classroom

Meet Kiev

Kiev is a nine-year-old boy in the fifth grade. He was born and raised in Cambodia until the age of seven. After spending some time in refugee camps, his family moved to California where they temporarily resided with cousins. Kiev was placed in the public school system, but his education was disrupted three times when his family had to relocate to look for employment. Over the summer, the family moved into our school area and purchased a doughnut shop. They plan on remaining here permanently (if the business works out). Kiev is resuming his education in the fifth grade with his age appropriate peers.

Kiev's mother speaks very little English. His dad does most of the translating, but he is at work seven days a week and is rarely home. Both parents were very involved in Kiev's education during the early years in Cambodia because school was and is very important to them. Since they have been in this country, however, his mother feels unable to participate in Kiev's education because of the language barrier. She attended an Open House at school and was also with us for our first class family meeting of the year. Prior to the start of school, she brought Kiev by the classroom to introduce herself and Kiev, and to show Kiev the room and the school in general. She was accompanied by Kiev's eighteen-month-old sister and a couple of cousins visiting from California that spoke English fluently.

In class, Kiev is very comfortable and fluent with regular conversation and slang. He participates in all class activities. He enjoys reading and writing workshop, but his work in writing is limited. Kiev is not comfortable writing and states so. It is difficult and time consuming for him. He is inhibited by his written abilities in English—particularly spelling. He also doesn't like the way he creates fantasy because the stories about what he knows are not pleasant. One of the first stories he chose to dictate to me was about his neighbors being shot down in the street as they went out to play with their new toys on Christmas morning. The second story he shared was about eating rats.

In reading, Kiev is participating in the same literature discussion groups as his classmates and appears to like the social context. Independently he chooses to read Shel Silverstein, comic books, baseball cards, Big Books, picture books, and Dr. Seuss books. We use these same materials when he and I work together on strategies and reading behaviors. Kiev has a good sense of humor and works casually, yet diligently, on most of his projects and assignments. His performance is about three years behind grade expectations in regard to silent reading comprehension and writing ability. Considering that these two areas are the most employed formats used on our required assessment measures, Kiev will not look very smart on paper. I realize that I need to bring Kiev to child study to discuss ways in which we can support his learning.

I have had several impromptu conversations with Kiev's mother regarding his performance, but have asked for a more formalized meeting where we can quietly discuss his work. I also want to familiarize his family with the procedures and rationale behind the child study meetings so they are not unnecessarily alarmed or confused.

The following scenario and questions were the results of a meeting with Kiev's parents. How would you respond?

Scenario: It is the day of your meeting. The children have gone home, and Kiev's parents have arrived. After discussing your observations and work samples, his parents have several questions.

1. What is a learning disability?
2. What is the difference between a reading disability and a learning disability?
3. Does Kiev qualify for ESOL or LEP services? What is the difference?
4. How can you be sure that Kiev has a learning disability and it's not just because of his language or culture?
5. What is the difference between mainstreaming and inclusion?

These are just some of the questions that may come up and in which we need to be prepared. If these answers are not clear in our minds, we cannot be doing the best for our students. The federal documents we read about in Chapter 2 inform us about the law, the intent, and our accountability as teachers. They establish our responsibilities and the rights of our children.

They don't easily answer the questions posed by Kiev's family. There is more we need to know in order to make informed decisions about our students, our students' learning, and the nature of language and literacy in general. The law is just the tip of the iceberg. Let's begin by looking at the correct legal responses to Kiev's parents.

Question 1 What is a learning disability?

Answer IDEA 97 defines a *specific learning disability* as a "disorder in one or more of the basic psychological processes involved in understanding or in using language, spoken or written. This disorder may manifest itself in imperfect ability to listen, think, speak, read, write, spell, or do mathematical calculations."[1] This term "includes such conditions as perceptual disabilities, brain injury, minimal brain dysfunction, dyslexia, and developmental aphasia."[2] This "term does not include a learning problem that is primarily the result of visual, hearing, or motor disabilities, of mental retardation, of emotional disturbance, or of environmental, cultural, or economic disadvantage."[3]

This is the federal definition that all schools and educators must use in determining a learning disability.

Question 2 What is the difference between a reading disability and a learning disability?

Answer When reading achievement is significantly below expectancy for both a student's chronological age and potential, the student is said to have a reading disability.[4]

Question 3 Does Kiev qualify for ESOL or LEP services, and what is the difference?

Answer Kiev will need to take a test, determined by the district, to see if he qualifies as an ESOL or LEP student. ESOL (English for/to Speakers of Other Language) is an academic program established to teach English language skills in an English speaking community or country to students whose first language is not English.[5] A child is usually referred for ESOL testing if they do not speak, write, read, or understand English; and their native language is not English.

An LEP student is a child who has a Limited English Proficiency. This term is used mostly with bilingual children[6] and refers to a student who has a restricted understanding or use of written and spoken English.

Question 4 How do you know if he has a learning disability and it's not just a language or cultural issue?

Answer It is required that all children be tested for services in their native language. Kiev speaks Cambodian and English. Because he was born in Cambodia and has only been in this country for two years, his English is limited and weak. It is required that he be tested for a learning disability in Cambodian. The school district will need to locate an individual who reads and writes Cambodian to administer the test, or to work with the special education department to help translate and analyze Kiev's reading comprehension and written expression as well as specific knowledge.

Question 5 What is the difference between mainstreaming and inclusion?

Answer Again, there is no single definition for the terms inclusion and mainstreaming. Inclusion is defined as the process and practice of educating students with disabilities in the general education classrooms of their neighborhood school.[7] When a child, with or without disabilities, is educated in the general education setting, they are educated in the *mainstream*. When a child *with* disabilities receives *some* of their education in the general classroom setting, then they are considered *mainstreamed*. The word *mainstreaming* implies that a student receives a part of his or her education in a separate, self-contained special education classroom and part of their education in a regular classroom setting. It would be accurate to refer to mainstreaming as *partial inclusion*.

If Kiev qualifies for special education services, and his IEP team determines that his educational needs can be met in the regular classroom on a full-time basis, and he remains in my classroom full time, then he is being educated in the mainstream and is considered to be a student of *inclusion*. If Kiev's IEP team determines that his academic and social needs cannot be met solely in the regular classroom, then he will only receive that instruction deemed appropriate in our room. Other parts of his education will be received outside of the mainstream in a special education classroom or resource room. In this situation, he is considered to be a student of *partial inclusion*. *Partial inclusion* is also known as *mainstreaming* or as moving towards or providing *inclusive education*.

For the remainder of this chapter, we will elaborate upon our responses to Kiev's parents and discuss some of the most common questions, issues, and concerns that arise when supporting children in our classrooms. After addressing the five main issues that apply to Kiev, we will look at some of the other terminology and concerns that you will encounter. We'll start with learning disabilities.

Learning Disabilities

The term *learning disabilities* is frequently misinterpreted.[8] In a recent review of literature, I found at least twelve[9] different definitions. Because each state is left to determine its own operational definition of learning disabilities, they are varied. This also means that a child may be Learning Disabled (LD) in one state and not in another.[10] While the law and regulations specify areas of deficits that constitute learning disabilities, there are widespread problems with the definition and the methods for identifying the individuals to be served.[11] In an analysis of the varied definitions, it was found that there were four factors that reoccurred in some definitions of LD—but not all. These factors were[12]

1. IQ-achievement discrepancy
2. presumption of central nervous system dysfunction
3. psychological processing disorders
4. learning problems not due to environmental disadvantage, mental retardation, or emotional disturbance

Kiev could be considered learning disabled with an IQ-achievement discrepancy, meaning that he is not achieving to his potential as measured by a standardized intelligence test. In other words, he would be failing to achieve at the level of his or her tested academic abilities.

However, the use of the IQ test as a fixed, valid method of determining a child's ability has created much controversy.[13] IQ does not remain stagnant; and the ten point discrepancy between IQ and achievement is in itself known to be a random number chosen for the purposes of identifying a cut-off point.[14] The standardized tests used to determine the achievement and placement have also been highly criticized for their lack of reliability as well as validity.[15] Regardless of the validity of the measures, in order to use this criteria as an accurate determiner of a learning disability, there would have to be a one-to-one linear relationship between intelligence test scores and scores on achievement tests. Research, however, shows this is not accurate.[16]

The other most commonly cited symptom of a learning disability is the presence of a perceptual disorder, such as an auditory or visual disorder.[17] Advocates of this view assume that a child having difficulty learning to read has problems in perceiving and integrating visual information.[18] Numerous studies have looked at the relationship between learning difficulties and perceptual measures and also have not yet yielded promising data.[19]

It was noted that among the children studied, many of the low achieving children displayed behaviors similar to those children known to have brain damage.[20] These characteristics included distractibility, hyperactivity, and perceptual disturbances. Professionals began to accept the notion that learning disabled individuals could also have a central nervous dysfunction, such as that evident in children with brain dysfunction. Now, assuming that learning disabled children have intrinsic learning problems because of a central nervous dysfunction, most definitions of learning disabilities must exclude those children whose problems stem from environmental disadvantage, mental retardation, or emotional disturbance. Although it is agreed that learning disabilities can occur along with environmental disadvantage, mental retardation, and emotional disturbance, for children to be considered learning disabled, their problems must primarily be the result of their learning disability[21] and not another handicap.

Upon looking at the term *learning disabled*, a national task-force found at least ninety-nine documented characteristics (or symptoms) of learning disabilities in the literature.[22] Using these characteristics, they narrowed down the symptoms into the top ten most frequent identifiers of a learning disability:[23]

1. hyperactivity
2. perceptual-motor impairments
3. emotional liability: frequent mood shifts
4. general coordination deficits
5. disorders of attention
6. disorders of memory and thinking
7. specific academic problems
8. difficulty in the area of reading, writing, math, and/or spelling
9. disorders of speech and hearing
10. equivocal neurological signs and EEG irregularities

It is stated that given the wide range of characteristics employed in classifying learning disabilities, more than 80 percent of all school-age children could be classified as learning disabled.[24] Based upon the documentation of children already classified as learning disabled and those not, researchers found that experienced educators could not tell the difference.[25] Because of the flexibility in definitions and unreliable assessments, some professionals believe that we really have no reliable way to distinguish between children with organic learning problems and children that just need different or more instruction in school.[26]

A learning disability implies the presence of a neurological disorder.[27] Yet, when a blind study was conducted in which LD students were compared with students who were deemed academically successful, there were no neurological differences found between the LD group and the non-LD group. All children classified as neurologically normal or abnormal did not differ in their neurological status.[28] Another study found that many children classified as learning disabled were not organically disabled; they were merely having difficulty learning to read. When these same LD children were placed in different learning situations where they developed various reading strategies,[29] they were reading at the average level of their peers within thirteen weeks.

Today, 50 percent of all special education and 5 percent of all school enrollment are learning disabled.[30] It was found that many teachers refer children for special education assistance based upon their need for additional help with the child, rather than any specific characteristic that the child has demonstrated.

Reading Disability and Learning Disability

The terms *reading disability* and *learning disability* are often used interchangeably. Because Kiev is functioning below expectations in reading for his age and potential, he has a reading disability. If Kiev is tested and also exhibits a ten point discrepancy between his IQ and his performance, or if he has a perceptual disorder, then he is also learning disabled. We could say that he has a learning disability in reading. It was found that reading and language difficulties are the most common problems experienced by children labeled as learning disabled.[31]

Dyslexia

The most well-known term applied to reading disabilities is *dyslexia*. Dyslexia is a specific type of reading disability that refers to an inability or partial inability to read.[32] This reading problem occurs in children of average intelligence and hearing and is not due to sensory impairment, faulty instruction, mental retardation, economic situation, or lack of motivation. It is not seen as an *acquired* disability, but is presumed to be *congenital* or perhaps hereditary in nature. The problem is intrinsic rather than extrinsic. The most common characteristic of people deemed dyslexic is an inability to spell.

Some professionals object to the infusion of medical terminology, such as *congenital* or *acquired* disability when describing reading difficulties.[33] When we look for physical dysfunctions within children, we refer to it as the *search for pathology*.[34] This emphasis of searching for organic problems within a student places all of the responsibility for learning on the child.[35] It takes the pressure off teachers, and it ignores all of the outside factors that we know contribute to and inhibit a child's success.

The Search for Pathology We know that reading performance does not remain constant across time or materials. Reading is interactive and subject to variation. People fluctuate in their reading strategies and performance whenever they encounter various types of print material. My reading of picture books does not require as much of my concentration as a medical journal. My comprehension of the picture book is fairly accurate and my reading more fluent. My performance would look great on paper. However, if you were testing me on the medical book, I would look like a different reader. I'm sure it would take me longer to read, and my pronunciation would falter. I would score lower on the comprehension questions compared to the picture book, and it would take me a while to respond to the questions accurately. I would want to go back to the text to locate answers. Since I am not familiar or comfortable with medical jargon, I would not read as confidently or clearly.

You would most likely think that my poor performance was a result of my inability to handle the medical material. I don't think you would automatically assume that my failure to perform well was the result of an underlying brain dysfunction or neurological disturbance. It's important to recognize that while we recognize variation as a given trait among competent readers, we rarely allow for this same variation among less able readers.[36] If we were to view reading disability from the same perspective as reading ability, then the need to identify the disability is eliminated.

Throughout the years, many theories regarding the nature of dyslexia have emerged.[37] Although many causes have been posited, we still do not have conclusive research or a consistent set of symptoms to define the term.[38] Some educators feel that the term itself is misused. It is frequently applied synonymously and generically with the term *reading disability* to discuss all reading difficulties. Currently, the term *dyslexia* is acknowledged and used by some reading professionals—but not all.

Cultural Issues

As a classroom teacher, you will not have much input regarding the district's policies on testing bilingual children. It is your job to assure that the child is treated fairly and to know how to advocate on the student's behalf. You will need to be aware of your student's abilities and performances, as well as the ESOL and LEP procedures and assessments.

ESOL and LEP

ESOL and LEP assessments are handled by the school district or your particular school. It is your job to make sure that your children are tested in their native language. If there is doubt regarding the proficiency of the child's English, then test the child in both languages. There is no harm done. For Kiev to be truly learning disabled, he must test learning disabled in Cambodian—not English. If test results show that he is not learning disabled in his native language, then he does not have a neurological disorder and his reading problems must be a language issue.

It is said that special education assessments often neglect children's social or cultural lives. The tests utilized by special education are known to be culturally biased and reflect values imposed by white, upper-middle class families.[39] Kiev's differences in knowledge are viewed as weaknesses and incompetencies. It is your job is to make sure that appropriate questions are raised, and that your children are treated fairly and equitably by the system. Lack of cultural knowledge does not and should not reflect a disability.

Inclusion and Mainstreaming

It's interesting to note that federal document IDEA 97 does not include the term *inclusion*.[40] By mandating that all eligible students are entitled to a *free appropriate public education* (FAPE) in the *least restrictive environment* (LRE), inclusion is interpreted, inferred, and supported. It is evident that the U.S. Department of Education has an obvious preference for educating disabled students in regular classroom settings with appropriate aid and support.

Based on FAPE and LRE, if Kiev qualifies for services, he must be educated in the classroom with his nondisabled classmates to the fullest extent possible. That setting is his *least restrictive environment*. If Kiev is *included* in the regular classroom and it appears that this arrangement does not meet his needs, then he may require pull-out or separate placement instruction. If this occurs, all other placements must be documented and explained on his IEP. The reason that the regular classroom setting did not meet his needs must be stated. So, although IDEA 97 is not a specific mandate for inclusion, the LRE requirements certainly give adequate support for its practice.[41]

Teacher Responsibilities

If Kiev is mainstreamed, you need to be ready and committed to accept the responsibility for the learning accommodations and outcomes as detailed in his IEP. You need to believe that he can learn in your classroom. You need to prepare your classroom and students to receive him, and you must be able to work collaboratively with his parents and special education staff.[42]

You will need to have the knowledge to select and adapt curricula and instructional methods according to his individual needs, and to provide a variety of instructional techniques that support his learning style—as well as the other children in the classroom. You will need to feel comfortable documenting performance and behaviors, administering and deciphering various assessments, and planning instruction based upon observations and information. You will need established policies and procedures for monitoring his progress, grading, and testing results.

The National Joint Committee on Learning Disabilities has identified core competencies that they believe are essential for general education teachers who are working with children with learning disabilities.[43] These competencies are as follows:

- an overview of the scope and sequence of the curriculum from kindergarten through twelfth grade. Teachers should be well prepared in their subject area and understand the central concepts and tools of inquiry in these areas.
- teachers must be competent to teach word analysis, spelling, reading comprehension, and the writing process.
- successful collaboration requires an equal partnership, willingness to collaborate, good communication skills, cooperation among the participating teachers, adequate planning time, and administrative support.
- knowledge of current definitions and characteristics of individuals with learning disabilities and how these affect students' development and performance.

- knowledge of legal rights of the students, parents, and guardians as well as the responsibilities of teachers and schools regarding related services.
- knowledge of special education procedures.
- familiarity with commonly used assessment instruments.
- identify informally each child's strengths and weaknesses across developmental areas.
- use various formal and informal assessments.
- evaluate student performance on an ongoing basis.
- modify and adapt assessment tools to meet specific needs.
- use appropriate grading procedures.
- develop and implement lesson plans to meet students' unique needs (and IEP).
- demonstrate knowledge of the continuum of services and placements.
- plan and implement instruction collaboratively as needed.
- modify instruction for groupings.
- modify instruction for personal characteristics.
- adapt technology.
- integrate students with disabilities into the academic and social classroom community.
- model respect and acceptance.
- provide opportunities for meaningful social interaction.
- employ various classroom management techniques.
- facilitate all students in small and large group activities.
- understand the child's culture and community.
- develop an effective partnership between school and home.
- establish and maintain collegial relationships with school and community.

Discussion

More than 90 percent of all learning disability students are taught in regular education classrooms for some part of their school day.[44] It was found that when children and teachers were provided with necessary adequate support, many learning disabled students placed in inclusionary settings developed better self images, became less critical and more motivated, and recognized their own academic and social strengths more than their noninclusionary peers.[45] They had positive peer relationships and their social skills improved. Low achieving students showed academic and social skill improvements. Students appeared to gain a greater sense of self and a new appreciation of their own skills and accomplishments.[46] Therefore, many supporters of inclusion take the position that they have seen inclusion work and they believe that inclusion is the right thing to do.[47]

Remedial Programs Current research shows that we have not been successful in teaching our children who are deemed learning disabled.[48] Studies since the 1930s have consistently found that special education classes were less effective or showed no advantage over the regular classroom setting. Schooling in segregated handicapped-only classes often meant a long school bus ride to a distant school where the quality of the education was second-rate, "bereft of decent opportunities for parent-school collaboration, and lacking any semblance of the state-of-the-art teaching. In fact, the problem from the parents' perspective was not the degree of inclusion, but the lack of benefit (and in some cases, the clear harm) from special education in handicapped-only settings."[49]

Most of our LD students are still placed in academic programs that traditionally offer limited reading strategies and delayed instruction.[50] Research has found that exposing children to these types of slower programs offered little educational value and only ensured that the children would always remain behind their peers.[51] In fact, the available evidence suggests that participants in special education classes continue to fall farther behind their classmates as they proceed through their education.[52]

Special education curriculum functions under the view that knowledge is reducible to objective facts; teaching is the transmission of those facts; and learning is the accumulation of those facts.[53] In this view of literacy, there is only one right answer. In order to accomplish this, special education teachers must operate predominately in the mode of direct instruction where *mastery* can be easily measured.[54] However, recent studies show that students taught using this model "...are far more proficient in regurgitating facts and performing at lower levels of cognition than in solving problems. Many can give short written answers to questions, but have difficulty writing a coherent paragraph. Some who have no difficulty recalling important dates and individuals cannot relate two events occurring in different places at different times...."[55]

In a comprehensive review of remedial programs, the remediation primarily involved individual worksheet tasks and children were rarely required to read more than one or two sentences at a time.[56] It was noted that the resource subskill curricula contained many isolated skill activities that kept the children from actually reading and/or writing. The time spent in skill and drill instruction was found not to increase their reading achievement. The resource techniques and materials utilized were imitations of regular classroom techniques that were slowed down and adapted to smaller group settings.[57]

Jackson[58] refers to this type of instruction as mimetic. Mimetic principles do not begin to cover all of the teaching situations that exist. Research shows that even very young children engage in complex reasoning tasks[59]— once thought beyond their ability. When schools force children to master basic skills or long lists of isolated subskills before they can be exposed to richer analytical processes, learning is hampered.[60] Routine practices, such as multiple choice and fill in the blanks are known to mask the persistence of children's misconceptions; and reducing isolated components to skill and drill exercises may actually make it harder for students to see connections. These drills often lead to knowledge, which is stored in the brain, but never used. Knowledge and skills taught in isolation, with little experience for application, are unlikely to ever be used outside the classroom.[61]

Mainstreaming and Pull-Out Services For the purposes of accommodating various needs, most LD students are mainstreamed. They do leave the classroom to receive services from a special education teacher at some point during the day. These type of pull-out classes are the most utilized remedial arrangements for LD students. However, with the passage of IDEA 97 and the implementation of the IEP requirements, we should see less pull-out instruction and more work towards inclusion. Educators will now be required to explain why the student is being removed from the classroom to meet their social and academic needs.

Part of the concern about pull-out services was that they tended to form a type of ability grouping within the tracking of special education. Pull-out services should not be confused with individual instruction; they are not the same.[62] Pull-out classes were found to devote a large portion of instructional time to rote learning (the lowest cognitive level of knowing).[63] The children in attendance all generally understood that they were the "dumb class".[64] Although tracking is usually advocated with good intentions it delivers inferior instruction, lowers self-esteem, reinforces negative stereotypes, and reproduces social hierarchies.[65] Statistics tell us that six out of ten special education placements of white students are in the gifted and talented programs;[66] whereas only one in ten black students qualify for such placement. Black children are three times as likely as white children to be placed in classes for the educable mentally retarded. And today's special education classes predominately consist of children living in low economic situations who are members of a racial minority. Most of these children are also male.

There is also evidence that pull-out instruction simply does not work.[67] It was found to result in inconsistent, disjointed, interrupted school days[68] created by a lack of curricular coordination, different paradigms, different objectives, different behavior expectations, and contrasting teaching styles that tend to confuse rather than complement. The shared responsibility for special education students usually resulted in administrative loss and shifting responsibility. No one was really accountable for the child.[69] The following list consists of other problematic areas that were identified.

- Special education placements did not address the immediate cause of the referral. It removed the child from the experience and training deemed necessary to teach them how to perform in a regular classroom.

- Negative effects of segregation, stereotyping, alienation, and discrimination were commonly reported among pull-out students.

- Pull-out programs reinforced a perception that students were slow or failing and affected teacher expectations.

- Pupils who did not fit in, performed poorly, were unlikeable, or problematic frequently became labeled as handicapped pupils and were pulled out for special education classes. Pull-out programs did little to alter this original difficulty of troublesome behavior.

- Pull-out programs did not provide the type of quality schooling that the students needed. Many of the students simply needed more instruction.

We are not providing children with opportunities to use their own common sense or form strategies for problem solving.[70] Instead, children are told what they need to know and how they need to learn it. As "blank slates" they quickly learn that they have absolutely nothing to offer in regards to their own education. So, while there are many people who support inclusion philosophically, some believe that not including children could have far more repercussions.

Opposition to Inclusion Some opposers of inclusion are concerned about what is known as the practice of *dump and hope*.[71] This is when a special education student is *dumped* into the mainstream classroom without adequate support and only the *hope* of success. Some fear that once the inclusionary student is *dumped* into the regular classroom, the district and school administrators will leave the details of *accommodation* up to the classroom teacher.

We will be responsible and accountable for figuring out what to do in our classrooms, and the special education teachers will be left trying to figure out how to satisfy all of these classroom teachers and students who are in need of in-class support and out-of-class meeting time.

It is also questionable as to whether the classroom teachers will actually receive the support they need from trained staff and classroom materials. At a minimum, there needs to be much coordinated planning time, opportunities for a great deal of small-group teaching within the classroom setting, and textbook materials written at several difficulty levels. If you are familiar with our schools you will recognize that this is a tall order.

Time for adequate planning and staff development are a rare commodity in public schools, yet *time* is seen as the key factor in all successful inclusionary models.[72] It is suggested that there be regular weekly planning times for all educators involved in the child's learning, resulting in approximately one to four (or more) hours of meeting time.[73] It is seen as essential that all educators working with the disabled student meet to discuss the child and the program. It is important to continuously and rigorously evaluate and review progress, make adjustments, write curriculum, and develop new strategies.[74] Finding time to do this adequately within the normal school day will be difficult—if not impossible.

Successful Inclusionary Factors Research shows that the most successful inclusionary models include the following three factors:[75]

- ongoing, appropriate staff development
- adequate support in the form of services, aids, accommodations, trained staff, materials, monies, and technology
- reduced class size

Title 1, Disadvantaged, At Risk, Low-Economic Status, Poverty, and More

Title 1 is a federally funded education program[76] aimed at serving children of lower socioeconomic status who may be at risk of school failure. Kiev, who may not qualify for a learning disability, may be eligible for services under Title 1 depending upon his family's socioeconomic status.

A child's *socioeconomic status* is determined by such factors as the family's social class, household income, level of education, and type of job.[77]

At Risk

A child is considered to be *at risk* if their prospects for success are deemed marginal.[78] The at-risk student is viewed as being in jeopardy of failing to complete an adequate level of academic skills.[79] At-risk children are also referred to as *slower learners*.[80] Typically, these children have tested IQs between 70 and 89, and are approximately one and a half to two years behind their peers academically on most tested measures. They have generally been retained or administratively placed (socially promoted) to the next grade level at least once.[81] At-risk children typically do not qualify for special education services because there is not a demonstrated difference between their tested ability (IQ) and their achievement (performance). Commonly, the prominent criterion for having a learning disability is the presence of a ten point discrepancy between the IQ score and the tested ability. Children deemed at risk are usually said to be working up to their potential[82] and therefore show no discrepancy between these two scores.

Poverty as an Academic Variable

The number of children living in poverty in the United States increased from 16 percent in the late 1970s to 25 percent today. Characteristics of children deemed at risk include:[83]

- low achievement
- grade retention
- behavior problems
- poor attendance
- low socioeconomic status

Each of these factors highly correlates to the dropout rate in our country.[84]

The government has recognized that the most consistent characteristic among children deemed at risk is poverty. Something needs to be done about the children who are considered "falling between the cracks." With our current emphasis on higher academic standards resulting in a suppressed, skill-based curriculum, the outlook for many children of poverty is grim. It is expected that 40 percent of all children will live on Aid to Dependent Children (ADC) for at least one year before reaching the age of eighteen.[85] Our current education reform may actually increase the risk of many low achieving students unless these higher standards are accompanied by additional classroom resources.[86]

Remediation of Slower Learners

The biggest concern regarding programs established to remediate slower learners is that regular classroom teachers "excuse themselves from responsibility for the education of low achieving students."[87] Once a child is placed, it's common for the child's core reading and/or math instruction to become the sole responsibility of the remediating teacher. The regular classroom teacher does not concern himself as much with the Title 1 child's academics, knowing they have support. Attention is now focused on other students in need. However, most Title 1 students spend the majority of their school day in regular classroom settings rather than in support programs.[88] Therefore, we have a situation where once children are placed, students who are in need of the most instruction may actually receive less of it in the regular classroom where they spend the majority of their time.

Similar to special education, the unfavorable research on pull-out instruction has also led to an increased push for inclusionary models of instruction for Title 1 students. In this situation, an aide or Title 1 teacher comes into the classroom and works directly with the child.[89] Besides the added benefit of continuity of instruction and classroom community, this model of remediation is also said to best prepare the student for future classroom settings—if his instruction remains immersed. However, it is also criticized because most Title 1 remediation services (in class or pull-out models) are still administered in small group or one-on-one settings. Therefore, this model still does not prepare the student to work independently or function in whole group activities.

This focus on remediation also tends to lead to a lower level form of curriculum. It was found that the curriculum differed depending upon the socioeconomic status of the students and their families.[90] In the working-class school, work was defined as following procedures. The curriculum was controlling, mechanical, involved rote instruction, and little decision making or choice on the part of the child. In the middle-class school, work tasks were also usually mimetic in nature and did not require creative thought. Answers were usually found in books or by listening to the teacher. They were rarely generated by the student. As the economic status of the students rose, so did the expectation and request for increased analytical, creative, and individual thought. The children in the "executive elite" schools were seen as being given something that none of the other schools provided: they were not only acquiring symbolic capital (such as those children in "professional" schools), but were obtaining practice in the manipulation of these "socially legitimated tools." It was concluded that "these differences may not only contribute to the development in the children in each social class of certain types of economically significant relationships and not others, but would thereby help to *reproduce* this system of relations in society. In the contribution to the reproduction of unequal social relations lies a theoretical meaning and social consequence of classroom practice."[91]

In Rist's[92] report on student social class and teacher expectations, he found that our system of public education actually perpetuates what it is ideologically supposed to eradicate—"class barriers that result in inequality in the social and economic life of the citizenry." Not only did Rist's report help illuminate the concept of the self-fulfilling prophecy, but he also highlighted the insidious nature in which social class is taught and maintained. Children subliminally learn how to treat others, and learn what to expect from others, from people in various caste systems.

So again, by helping, we could be also be hurting.

ADD, ADHD

There's always one child in the class who cannot sit still. They fidget in their seats. They blurt out answers in the middle of questions. They make careless mistakes and avoid detail in their work. Their mind wanders. They daydream. Instructions and organizational skills are rarely followed through independently. They lose things. These are said to be the key characteristics of Attention Deficit Disorder, commonly referred to as ADD.[93]

ADHD (Attention Deficit Hyperactivity Disorder) is when a child demonstrates impulsive behaviors and an inability to concentrate, plus has a tendency to be hyperactive over a consistent period of time.[94] This child has a hard time waiting their turn in games or tasks. They cannot sit still and are generally more aggressive, disruptive, and obtrusive than the child with ADD.

There are an estimated 1.46 to 2.46 million children with ADD in the United States (approximately 35 percent of our school population).[95] Boys are diagnosed with ADD four to nine times more often than girls.[96] There remains no direct or conclusive test for ADD[97] and diagnosis is the main challenge. A lot of work has been done to inform and train practitioners in the medical field, but ADD is complex and much confusion remains about the disorder. ADD can also mimic or coexist with such problems as learning disabilities, anxiety, depression, hearing loss, sleep disorders, and epilepsy.

Some educators denounce ADD as a handy label that is too readily applied by parents, doctors, and teachers. Much of the critic's concern comes from the treatment, which usually takes the form of a pill. The most common of these medications is Ritalin. When the use of Ritalin doubled in the early 1990s questions regarding inappropriate use and diagnosis arose.[98]

If children with ADD do not qualify for special education services under Section B of IDEA 97, then they may be eligible for services under Section 504 of the Rehabilitation Act of 1973.[99] Depending upon the severity of the disorder, some ADD children may have a physical or mental impairment which substantially limits their learning (such as Molly in Chapter 2). If that is the case, then the law requires that the school make modifications or adaptations. The child must be educated in the regular classroom to the maximum extent possible, and all accommodations need to be made at the expense of the school. An IEP also needs to be written.

What's Next?

The federal documents speak to the law. They outline your obligations as a teacher and the rights of the children in your classroom. It is your job to advocate on your students' behalf and see that the law is applied fairly and equitably. To do this, you must be aware of the flexibility of the law, and make sure that the picture created by the federal documentation is an accurate representation of students in your classroom (Kiev for example). The special education department will take care of the quantitative side of Kiev's data to establish criteria. Your job is to fill in the rest of the picture, the qualitative side. You need to show the child study team Kiev, and what Kiev can do. They need to see how these numbers reflect his work in the classroom, and what he looks like beyond his tested abilities. They need to see how these numbers translate into his learning. Without your data, his test scores will be used as evidence of his placement, his developmental level, and his abilities. These numbers will then be used as a baseline to determine his curriculum, placement, and IEP goals. You must make sure that the picture of Kiev is accurate and just.

To do this, you need to be able to analyze Kiev's work samples and school behaviors. You need to search for evidence of literacy strengths that complete Kiev as a learner and inform everyone concerned of his performance. You need to isolate his literacies so that educators can speak to them specifically. But what does a literate person look like? Again, that very well may depend upon your definitions. What is learning? What is literacy? What is reading? We'll look at these issues in Chapter 4.

References

Algozzine, B. 1985. "Low Achiever Differentiation: Where's the Beef?" *Exceptional Children* 52: 72–75.

Allington, R. L. 1995. "Literacy Lessons in the Elementary Schools: Yesterday, Today, and Tomorrow." In R. Allington and S. A. Walmsley's, *No Quick Fix:* 19–44. Newark, DE: International Reading Association.

Allington, R. L., and McGill-Franzen, A. 1989. "Different Programs, Indifferent Instruction." In D. Lipsky and A. Gartner's, *Beyond Separate Education:* 3–32. NY: Brookes.

Anyon, J. 1981. "Social Class and the Hidden Curriculum of Work." In W. Pinar, H. Giroux, and A. N. Penna's *Curriculum and Instruction: Alternatives in Education:* 317–341. Berkeley, CA: McCutchan.

Beers, C., and Beers, J. W. 1980. "Early Identification of Learning Disabilities: Facts and Fallacies" *The Elementary School Journal* 81, no. 2: 579–586.

Bicklin, D., and Zollers, N. 1986. "The Focus of Advocacy in the LD Field" *Journal of Learning Disabilities* 26, no. 10: 579–586.

Bigelow, B. 1994. "Getting Off the Track: Stories from an Untracked Class" *Rethinking Classrooms, Teaching for Equity and Justice*: 58–65. Rethinking Schools, Ltd.

Cardenas, J., and McCarty First, J. 1985. "Children at Risk" *Educational Leadership* 43, no. 1: 4–8.

Clay, M. 1987. "Learning to Be Disabled" *New Zealand Journal of Educational Studies* 22, no. 2: 155–173.

Clements, S. D. 1966. "Minimal Brain Dysfunction in Children: Terminology and Identification" *NINDB* Monograph, no. 3, Washington, DC: U.S. Department of Health, Education, and Welfare.

Coles, G. S. 1978. "The Learning Disabilities Test Battery: Empirical and Social Issues" *Harvard Educational Review* 48, no. 3: 313–340.

Consumer Reports. 1997. "Your Health: When Kids Can't Concentrate, Attention Deficit Disorder" *Consumer Reports* February: 56.

Cunningham, P. M., and Allington, R. L. 1999. *Classrooms That Work: They Can Really Read.* NY: Longman.

Curry School of Education. 1998. "Inclusion" *Curry School of Education*: http://curry.edschool.virginia.edu/go...aled/information/uvald/inclusion.html.

Dyer, P. C., and Binkney, R. 1995. "Estimating Cost-Effectiveness and Educational Outcomes: Retention, Remediation, Special Education, and Early Intervention." In R. Allington and S. Walmsley's *No Quick Fix*: 61–77. Newark, DE: International Reading Association.

Gartner A., and Lipsky, D. K. 1987. "Beyond Special Education: Toward a Quality System for All Students" *Harvard Educational Review* 57, no. 57: 367–395.

Goodlad, J. I. 1984. *A Place Called School*. NY: McGraw-Hill Book Company.

Hallahan, D. P., and Kauffman, J. M. 1991. *Exceptional Children: Introduction to Special Education*. Boston: Allyn and Bacon.

Harris, T. L., and Hodges, R. E. 1995. *The Literacy Dictionary*. Newark, DE: International Reading Association.

Heumann, J. E., and Hehir, T. 1998. "Memorandum: Effective Dates of New IEP Requirements" *The Special Ed Advocate* April 28, http://www.wrightslaw.com/MORANDUM_IEP_980428.html.

Jackson, P. W. 1985. "Private Lessons in Public Schools: Remarks on the Limits of Adapted Instruction." In Wang and Walberg's *Adapting Instruction to Individual Differences*: 66–81. Berkeley, CA: McCuthcan.

Johnson, D. 1995. "Dyslexia." In Theodore L. Harris, and Richard E. Hodges's *The Literacy Dictionary*: 64–65. Newark, DE: International Reading Association.

Kavale, K. 1990. "A Critical Appraisal of Empirical Subtyping Research in Learning Disabilities." In H. Swanson and B. Keogh's *Learning Disabilities: Theoretical and Research Issues*: 215–222. Hillsdale, NJ: Lawrence Erlbaum Associates.

Kelly, E. J. 1971. *Philosophical Perspectives in Special Education*. Columbus, OH: Charles E. Merrill Publishing Company.

Kincheloe, J. L. 1993. *Toward a Critical Politics of Teacher Thinking: Mapping the Post Modern*. Critical Studies in Education and Culture Series. NY: Bergin and Garvey.

Lambert, M. 1984. "Teaching about Thinking and Thinking about Teaching" *Journal of Curriculum Studies* 16: 1–18.

Lightfoot, A. 1972. *Inquiries Into the Social Foundations of Education: Schools in Their Urban Setting*. Chicago: Rand McNally.

Lyons, C. 1989. "Reading Recovery: An Effective Program That Can Prevent Mislabeling of Children as Learning Disabled" *ERS Spectrum* 7: 3–9.

McKnight, T. R. 1986. "The Learning Disability Myth in American Education" *Journal of Education* 164, no. 4: 351–359.

McLaren, P. 1994. *Life in Schools: An Introduction to Critical Pedagogy in the Foundations of Education*. NY: Longman Publishing Group.

Moats, L.C., and Lyon, G. R. 1993. "Learning Disabilities in the United States: Advocacy, Science, and the Future of the Field" *Journal of Learning Disabilities* 26, no. 5: 282–294.

National Institute of Health. 1997. "Report on Learning Disabilities Research" *National Institute of Health*: July 10.
http://www.ldonline.org/ld_indepth/reading/nih_report.html.

NICHCY. 1995. "Planning for Inclusion" *National Information Center for Children and Youth with Disabilities* 5, no. 1, #ND24: July.

NJCLD. 1997. "Learning Disabilities: Preservice Preparation of General and Special Education Teachers" *National Joint Committee on Learning Disabilities* February 1.
http://www.ldonline.org/njcld/preservice_prep.html.

NJCLD. 1990. "Learning Disabilities: Issues on Definition" *National Joint Committee on Learning Disabilities* January.
http://www.ldonline.org/njcld/defn_91.html.

Nowell, R., and Innes, J. 1997. "Educating Children Who Are Deaf or Hard of Hearing: Inclusion" *ERIC Digest* ED414675 97, ERIC Clearinghouse on Disabilities and Gifted Education: Reston,VA.

Reynolds, M., and Wang, M. 1983. "Restructuring 'Special' School Programs: A Position Paper" *Policy Studies Review* 2: 189–212.

Ripley, S. 1997. "Collaboration Between General and Special Education Teachers" *ERIC Digest* ED 409317, Eric Clearinghouse on Teaching and Teacher Education, Washington, DC: July.

Rist, R. C. 1970. "Student Social Class and Teacher Expectations: The Self-Fulfilling Prophecy in Ghetto Education" *Harvard Educational Review* 40, no. 3: 411–455.

Rothman, R. 1991. "Scholars Seek to Forment 'Revolution' in Schools" *Education Week* October 9.

Shapiro, J., and Kilbey, D. 1990. "Closing the Gap Between Theory and Practice: Teacher's Belief's, Instructional Decisions, and Critical Thinking" *Reading Horizons* 31, no. 1: 59–73.

Shepard, L. A. 1994. "The Challenges of Assessing Young Children Appropriately" *Phi Delta Kappa* 76, no. 3: 206–212.

Shor, I. 1992. *Empowering Education*. Chicago: The University of Chicago Press.

Siegel, L. 1990. "I.Q. and Learning Disabilities." In H. Swanson and B. Keogh's *Learning Disabilities: Theoretical and Research Issues*: 111–130. Hillsdale, NJ: Lawrence Erlbaum Associates.

Skrtic, T. 1991. "The Special Education Paradox: Equity as the Way to Excellence" *Harvard Educational Review* 61: 148–206.

Slavin, R. E., and Madden, N. A. 1989. "What Works for Students at Risk: A Research Synthesis" *Educational Leadership* February: 4–13.

Smith, F. 1986. *Insult to Intelligence: The Bureaucratic Invasion of Our Classrooms*. Portsmouth, NH: Heinemann.

Stowell, L. P., and Tierney, R. J. 1995. "Portfolios in the Classroom: What Happens When Teachers Negotiate Assessment?" In R. L. Allington and S. A. Walmsley's *No Quick Fix*: 78–96. Newark, DE: International Reading Association.

Texas Education Agency. 1985. "The Slower Learner: An Advocate's View" [ED 346 685]. *Practioner's Guide Series, Number Two*. Austin, TX: Texas Dropout Information Clearinghouse.

U.S. Department of Education. 1994. "Attention Deficit Disorder: Adding Up the Facts" U.S. Department of Education. Washington, D.C.

Wallmsley, S. and Allington, R. L. 1995. "Redefining Reform and Reforming Instructional Support Programs for At Risk Students." In R. L. Allington and S. A. Walmsley's *No Quick Fix*: 19–44. Newark, DE: International Reading Association.

Withers, R., and Lee, J. 1988. "Power in Disguise." In L. Barton's *The Politics of Special Educational Needs*: 175–189. Hillsdale, NJ: Lawrence Erlbaum Associates.

Wittrock, M. 1986. *Handbook of Research on Teaching*. NY: Macmillan.

Ysseldyke, J., Algozzine, B., Shinn, M., and McGue, M. 1982. "Similarities and Differences Between Low Achievers and Students Classified as LD" *The Journal of Special Education* 16: 73–84.

Notes

1. IDEA 97, Subchapter I, Sec. 1401. (26)(A).
2. IDEA 97, Subchapter I, Sec. 1401. (26)(B).
3. IDEA 97, Subchapter I, Sec. 1401. (26)(C).

4. Harris and Hodges, 1995.

5. Harris and Hodges, 1995; Hallahan and Kauffman, 1991.

6. Harris and Hodges, 1995; Hallahan and Kauffman, 1991.

7. Nowell and Innes, 1997. Note: A child's neighborhood school is the school that the child would attend if they didn't have a disability.

8. NJCLD, January, 1990 Learning Disabilities: Issues on Definition.

9. LD On Line (http://www.ldonline.org/ccldinfo/1.html); NJCLD, January, 1990 Learning Disabilities: Issues on Definition; Gartner and Lipsky, 1987; Biklen and Zollers, 1986; Hallahan and Kauffmann, 1991.

10. Moats and Lyons, 1993.

11. NJCLD, January, 1990 Learning Disabilities: Issues on Definition.

12. Hallahan and Kauffmann, 1991.

13. Clay, 1987; Kavale, 1990; Siegel, 1990; Lightfoot, 1972.

14. Texas Education Agency, 1989.

15. Stowell and Tierney, 1995; Withers and Lee, 1988; McKnight, 1986; Beers and Beers, 1980; Shepard, 1994; McLaren, 1994; Coles, 1978; Moats and Lyon, 1993.

16. McKnight, 1986.

17. McKnight, 1986.

18. Hallahan and Kauffmann, 1991.

19. McKnight, 1986.

20. Now called brain dysfunction, Hallahan and Kauffmann, 1991.

21. Hallahan and Kauffmann, 1991.

22. Clements, 1966.

23. Hallahan and Kauffmann, 1991.

24. Gartner and Lipsky, 1987; Biklen and Zollers, 1986.

25. Algozzine, 1985; Ysseldyke et al., 1982; Gartner and Lipsky, 1987.

26. Dyer and Binkney, 1995.

27. McKnight, 1986.

28. McKnight, 1986.

29. Reading Recovery.

30. Lyons, 1989.

31. Kuder, 1991.

32. Harris and Hodges, 1995; Hallahan and Kauffman, 1991.

33. Johnson, 1995.

34. Wixson and Lipson, 1986.

35. Biklin and Zollers, 1986; Skrtic, 1991.

36. Wixson and Lipson, 1986, p. 131.

37. Johnson, 1995

38. Johnson, 1995.

39. McLaren, 1994.

40. NICHCY, 1995 (updated their introduction in 1997; text remains the same).

41. NICHCY, 1995.

42. ERIC Clearinghouse on Disabilities and Gifted Education (ED358677; July 1993).

43. NJCLD, February 1, 1997.

44. The Curry School of Education. Note: 1998 approximates this number at 80 percent.

45. Ripley, 1997.

46. Ripley, 1997.

47. NICHCY, 1995.

48. The Handbook of Research on Teaching, Wittrock, 1986.

49. U.S. Supreme Court: Brown v. Board of Education.

50. Walmsley and Allington, 1995.

51. Allington, 1995, p. 8; Lyons, 1989.

52. Walmsley and Allington, 1995.

53. Shapiro and Kilbey, 1990.

54. Kincheloe, 1993.

55. Goodlad, 1984, p. 299

56. Allington and McGill-Franzen, 1989.

57. Kelly, 1971.

58. 1985.

59. Rothman, 1991; Smith, 1986.

60. Rothman, 1991.

61. Rothman, 1991.

62. Goodlad, 1984.

63. Bigelow, 1994.

64. Bigelow, 1994.

65. Bigelow, 1994; McLaren, 1994; Goodlad, 1984; Shor, 1992.

66. McLaren, 1994.

67. Biklin and Zollers, 1986.

68. Reynolds and Wang, 1983.

69. Biklin and Zollers, 1986.

70. Lampert, 1984; Rothman, 1991.

71. NICHCY, 1995.

72. ERIC Clearinghouse on Disabilities and Gifted Education, 1993; Ripley, 1997; NICHCY, 1995.

73. ERIC Clearinghouse on Disabilities and Gifted Education, 1993; Ripley, 1997; NICHCY, 1995.

74. Ripley, 1997.

75. ERIC Clearinghouse on Disabilities and Gifted Education, 1993; Ripley, 1997; NICHCY, 1995.

76. Harris and Hodges, 1995.

77. Harris and Hodges, 1995.

78. Harris and Hodges, 1995.

79. Slavin and Madden, Feb. 1989.

80. The Texas Education Agency, 1989.

81. The Texas Education Agency, 1989.

82. The Texas Education Agency, 1989.

83. Slavin and Madden, Feb. 1989.

84. Slavin and Madden, Feb. 1989.

85. Cunningham and Allington, 1999.

86. Cunningham and Allington, 1999; Cardenas and First, 1985.

87. Allington and Walmsley, 1995.

88. Allington and Walmsley, 1995.

89. Slavin and Madden, 1989.

90. Anyon, 1981.

91. Anyon, 1981, p. 339.

92. 1970, p. 449.

93. U.S. Dept. of Education, 1994; National Institute of Health, 1993.

94. U.S. Dept. of Education, 1994.

95. U.S. Dept. of Education, 1994.

96. U.S. Dept. of Education, 1994.

97. Consumer Reports, February, 1997.

98. Consumer Reports, February, 1997.

99. U.S. Dept. of Education, 1994.

4

Understanding Literacy and Learning

Putting It to Work

What does it mean to be literate? What does a good reader look like? How do we define reading? To answer these questions, let's look at our own literacy behaviors.

1. You have just returned home from a busy day at work. Your primary goal is to kick off your shoes and relax. You put on some soft music, pour a glass of wine, change into comfortable clothes, and decide to spend some time reading. You:
   a. Write some spelling words three times each
   b. Complete the worksheet page on pronouns
   c. Alphabetize your grocery list
   d. Practice the sounds of short a
   e. Read a novel

2. When reading a book you:
   a. Read the book out loud
   b. Know every word
   c. Stop to journal your predictions and outcomes along the way
   d. Summarize the main events of each chapter in writing
   e. Enjoy the story

3. When finished reading, you:
   a. Write a book report
   b. Create a pictoral time line of the story's main events
   c. Give yourself a vocabulary test
   d. Make a diorama
   e. Share it with a friend or put the book away

What Is Reading?

In our adult lives we read to make sense of our world: to learn, to communicate, to navigate, to broaden our ideas, to enjoy... Our reading takes on a function and a relevancy in our lives. Usually we read for a specific purpose: reading a map when entering a new locale, monitoring the gas tank in our car, cramming for a test, locating phone numbers and addresses in the Yellow Pages, reading a TV guide, dreaming over vacation brochures, catching up on the morning headlines, balancing the bank statement, or simply escaping in biographies or mysteries. Reading takes on meaning.

In school, reading usually looks much different. Many of the reading materials employed in the classroom are not materials that we read or utilize outside of school. There is little free choice or authentic involvement with print for personal reasons and exploration. A good reader in school would be a student that completed all of the school's required reading assessments successfully. One of the main purposes of school instruction is to help create and support literacy so that all of our children may learn to function as productive, responsible citizens.

However, as we saw in Chapter 1, the ability to successfully pass many of these informal reading tests, worksheets, and standardized measures did not necessarily mean that my children could read. The children in my high reading group successfully completed comprehension tests, worksheets, sight word lists, phonic and phonemic awareness activities, spelling tests, and formal standardized measures. They looked extremely strong on paper. Yet, many of these students were unable to pick up the book they were tested on and actually read a story without assistance. And then there are situations, such as Kiev's, where a child demonstrates literacy behaviors in the classroom, but these strengths are not captured in formal assessments.

What Is Literacy?

Literacy is seeing yourself as a reader and choosing to interact with print.[1] When Kiev asked to participate in a literature discussion group, which required a lot more effort and time than he normally liked to apply, I knew that he would be okay with his learning that year. I know that once any child chooses to participate and share their readings and writings, they will increase their reading skills. I can work and support a child at any level in their learning, but I can't do it without their willingness and determination. Having a child *want* to read and learn makes my job so much easier. Whenever a child interacts with print, they are continuously and independently using reading strategies and applying skills. Regardless of the grade level assigned to the material, they are choosing appropriate independent reading material and practicing with print. Kiev now realizes that print can be flexible and fun. He enjoys reading and writing. He is taking responsibility and risks, developing a flexible repertoire of strategies for constructing meaning, monitoring comprehension, and solving problems. Through his readings and sharing, he is gaining information and insight into himself as well as others. He is bonding and finding acceptance and common ground among his peers. He's developing increasingly sophisticated and flexible strategies for generating ideas, drafts, revising, editing, and publishing. He is developing an appreciation for different kinds of literature as well as using the conventions of various literature genres in his writing. So, whenever I cannot be directly there for Kiev, I can breathe easier knowing that he is continuously thinking and creating with print. Practice makes perfect, and the only way to practice reading and writing is to read and write. Kiev's request is just one of those student moments you wait for and celebrate—it is a literacy event.

What Is Learning?

Kiev's learning is self-motivated, social, and personal. What do you remember about elementary school?

> What did your elementary school look like?
>
> Who was your first grade teacher?
>
> What was the best thing you ever did in grade school? Why was it so neat?

- I went to school in a great seven-story brick building. There was a wrought-iron fire escape, which coiled it's way around the outside of the walls to our classroom windows.
- In the first grade, my teacher's name was Mrs. Brewer. I made a beautiful pink gumdrop tree out of a real stick and threw up during our school play. I was Little Miss Muffit.

- In the third grade, I couldn't write very well with the new ink pens they made us use. I also cried in class one day because I couldn't weave my potholder and everybody else was finished.
- The best thing that ever happened to me was when I was in the fourth grade. I entered a school poetry contest. We were supposed to write about a giant paper-mache rabbit that the art teacher created. The winner was going to receive six creme-filled chocolate eggs, and the poem would be posted on the bulletin board outside the front office! When my poem *Floppy* won, I knew there was something I could do well.

Learning is so very social and personal. I need to create a curriculum that remembers what it's like to be a child. I need to support my children emotionally so that I can support them academically. The curriculum must support learning, evidence of growth, and implement all of the required content. In order to individualize, I need to create a program that is fairly adaptable, autonomous, flexible, and open-ended. Based upon these requirements there are some constants, regardless of the grade level that I am teaching, that provide some structure and support. My program will always:

- be a student-centered, hands-on learning environment utilizing a variety of instructional groupings and structures, which remain flexible and dependent upon intent.
- employ a variety of teaching styles and materials.
- begin with a shared reading period that includes concepts I want the class to experience, practice, share, appreciate, and/or discuss. The materials for this period will be generated by our content of study or student interest and will be supported by our morning picture book and poem. Daily language arts activities will include forms of shared reading, teacher read aloud time, independent reading, oral and silent reading, free writing, and writing to a prompt or direction.
- include some form of writing workshop and responding to literature.
- incorporate an inquiry-based format and be taught through literature to the extent of resources available in the content areas of math, social studies, and science.

Given these known strategies and techniques, I merely need to adapt the curriculum to my given grade level and content, and figure out how I want to incorporate the remaining material and academic elements.

Coming Together in the Classroom

Schedule

8:15–8:30	Morning procedures: putting away supplies, visiting with classmates
8:30–9:00	Morning journals and sharing time
9:00–9:30	Shared reading time
9:30–11:00	Reading/writing workshop
11:00–11:30	Lunch
11:30–12:00	Teacher read aloud time
12:00–12:45	Math
12:45–2:00	Inquiry study
2:00–2:45	Special activity (PE, Music, etc.)
2:45–3:00	Dismissal

A Typical Day

Our morning begins at the sound of the first bell at 8:15. The children enter the classroom, greet their classmates, organize their supplies, and ready themselves for the school day. When the second bell rings, the children take their morning journals to their seat and begin writing and drawing. I take care of all my secretarial duties and by the time the morning announcements have concluded, the children have generally completed their journal entries and have shared them at their table or with the class. At this point, we move to our carpet area for a morning of shared reading.[2]

Shared Reading Each day begins with what I refer to as our shared reading time. Regardless of the grade, K–6, we begin each day with a picture book. The picture book usually doubles as enjoyment reading for discussion, as well as reinforces or generates some concepts, skills, reading strategies, personal interests, or content knowledge. After reading and enjoying the book, we discuss all or parts of it and continue using the book in a mini-lesson type format, or reserve the option of returning to it later. The picture book is followed by our morning poem.

The purpose of the morning poem is to introduce and sustain poetry as a genre, as well as provide a different type of print to elicit reader response and reinforce comprehension strategies. In the primary grades of K–2, the

poem generally changes each week and is teacher selected. It is usually written on chart paper or sentence strips and displayed for repeated readings. In
the beginning of the school year, I illustrate the poem for the class. We spend
time throughout the year discussing illustrations and identifying the author's
words that created those illustrations in our minds. As the year progresses,
the children take turns illustrating the poem.

We also utilize the weekly poem in games, such as *Hang Man* or *Wheel
of Fortune*. We examine and share the things we notice about the poem in a
game of *I Spy*. The children identify letters they know, find word families,
create new words by changing or removing letters, recognize like sounds and
parts of classmates' names, locate rhyming words, name and notice conventions of print, and read familiar words. The children also receive a copy of
the poem to illustrate and place in their poem book, which is read and maintained throughout the year.

In the intermediate grades, a new poem is chosen and discussed daily.
Sometimes it is placed on chart paper. Other times it is viewed on an overhead transparency, sentence strips, or poster board. At the beginning of the
year, I illustrate our daily poem. Shortly into the school year, the helper for
the day is responsible for choosing the poem, illustrating the poem, and sharing it with the class. The helper is also the first person to share something that
they notice about the poem or the printed text. They then call on a couple of
classmates to share their observations and comment on the poem. Some children share their own poetry at this time. In the third grade, I have used both
procedures, a weekly poem and/or a daily poem depending upon my intent
and the composition of my class. At the end of our shared reading time, we
move into reading workshop and writing workshop for the remainder of the
morning until lunch. Before leaving our shared reading time, a status check
for writing workshop is taken. This is explained in the next section.

Writing Workshop Writing workshop typically consists of free writing time
and includes letters, fiction, nonfiction, recipes, posters, advertisements,
newspaper articles, poetry, calendars, and so on. There have also been times
when the children have responded to a certain teacher prompt or an assignment during writing workshop time. This usually occurs if I need to focus the
children on learning to write to a prompt or if there is a class activity that
needs to be completed, such as an essay on being drug free for DARE or
working on class books or projects. Otherwise, I like to maintain writing
workshop as strictly for creative purposes of writers' choice.

The rules for writing workshop do not vary much between the grade
levels. All of the children are required to:

- write daily
- date every page
- erase nothing
- keep all drafts

My job is to observe and monitor the writing behaviors, attitudes, growth, and performance of my students. During writing time, I walk around and talk briefly with the students about their writing. Sometimes we may have an impromptu conference regarding their story and where they're going with it. Sometimes we may work on a form of convention like indenting paragraphs, using quotations, punctuation, or capital letters. Maybe we'll look at adding colorful language and search for adjectives to make their writing more engaging and entertaining. Periodically we will have formal writing conferences where I sit with the child and their writing notebook and we assess growth and establish goals. I am constantly reviewing each child's development of their writing and writing processes to see where we can continue to improve their skills.

As stated earlier, I take a status check of the class at the end of our shared reading time to determine what each child intends to work on during writing workshop. This forces the child to commit to some form of work with print before leaving our group time. It also allows me the opportunity to stay informed of what my students are involved in and how they are experimenting in their writing. This is also a good opportunity to commend those students who utilize various stages of the writing process, and encourage others who don't to do so. It allows me to use the vocabulary associated with authoring, such as drafting and/or illustrating. I can discuss what is meant by editing. "Are you editing or revising?" I can see which children experiment with various forms of print and which do not. It also serves as a work contract between the student and me.

After the status check, every child leaves the carpet area and retrieves their writing workshop notebook. In grades three and higher their notebook is a three-ring, loose-leaf binder containing lined notebook paper. In the primary grades, I tend to use various bound books containing newsprint or portfolio type envelopes. In second grade, I try to move the children (depending upon the level of each child) to notebooks rather than bound books by mid-year. This motivates them to accept the added responsibility of keeping their work together and to move along in their writing.

The students start by finding a writing area they are comfortable with and begin to work. Sometimes we start our writing workshop with a quiet/silent time of ten minutes to allow everyone to focus and become engaged before they begin shuffling around and talking. At times, children like this writing time to be really quiet for the entire duration. Classical or nature music usually plays softly in the background while the children go about their business. We follow this routine as closely as possible Monday through Friday.

Reading Workshop Once all of the children are involved in their writing, I focus my attention more to the area of reading. Reading workshop, for me, consists of literature discussion groups, small group instruction, some one-on-one instruction, and always assessment and observation. Each of these methods may be implemented and look differently depending upon the developmental level of the learner, allowing accommodation for my various needs.

Developing readers—those that are not yet autonomous reading print—will need different instruction and support than a reader who is highly independent and flexible in both their reading materials and strategies. Typically these are reading behaviors found in grades K–2 and tend to taper off in the third grade. However, there are many children in the higher grades that are also developing readers and need the same kind of support and reading instruction as children in the primary grades. Therefore, as a teacher you need to be prepared to teach basic reading strategies utilizing various types of print to all children regardless of age and stage of development.

It is important that all children learn strategies for solving unfamiliar or new words and phrases and be immersed in a variety of literacy opportunities. Once a child is functioning at an independent stage of reading, teachers can then spend more time with other needy readers.

Literature Groups The purpose of literature groups is to:

- discuss literature
- respond to literature (orally and through print)
- read aesthetically
- take responsibility
- internalize reading by relating it to the child's own life
- verbalize and share ideas in a small group setting
- learn the art of conversation
- be exposed to various perspectives, ideas, and ways of thinking
- practice reading strategies using various forms of print
- address conventions of print, vocabulary, and elements of a story that arise in the text

In grades two through six, literature groups run approximately three weeks per book and include three books per quarter. During this time, I choose five or six related books[3] and briefly introduce them[4] to the children. The children peruse the books and decide which book they would like to read during the next group time. In literature group, the children sit in a circle while reading the same book and discuss what they have read and/or their impressions of the story. They maintain a reading journal, which they bring to each group meeting to use to share their responses. We discuss aspects of the story, their observations, or perhaps engage in a brief focus lesson on a topic or issue from the text or our conversation. We may do all three. The children are evaluated on all aspects of performance including reading, sharing, listening, and writing in their journals. Using these assessments and observations, I am able to see the confidence and capability with which the children articulate, comprehend, and internalize print. When we have progressed through the story and the book has been completed (approximately three weeks), the children know that they are required to turn in their journals for grading. They also take some type of open-ended reading test covering the content of the book and are expected to create and present a project based on their readings.

When the children receive their new reading book they receive a gallon-sized, Zip-lock plastic bag and a reading contract. The reading contract (also referred to as literature contracts) is used as my main organizational structure. Literature contracts vary in appearance according to their need and intent, but they always take on the form of a calendar or planner. They are used for the purposes of tracking reading assignments, due dates for each literature book, reading tests, journal grades, and projects required in a reading group. The reading contract is an agreement between myself and the reader. It is perfect for students who are out sick or going to be away for any length of time because it provides the child with reading assignments as well as other expectations for the month. There is little confusion concerning make-up work or assignment due dates. It also helps children who participate in after school activities, such as sports, which may interfere with homework time, determine what is expected of them. The children know what is assigned in advance and can pace themselves accordingly. The reading contracts are signed by myself, the student, and the parent.

The children keep their reading book and reading contract in their gallon bag. At the beginning of the school year, they are each given a bookmark and a spiral-bound notebook to maintain as their reading journal. They receive a list of over forty options to choose from for writing in their journal, which includes a personal choice, and a package of Post-it notes in case they want to mark pages, mark sections, or mark vocabulary they found interesting or confusing. The journal, the suggested journal choices, the bookmark, and the Post-it notes also fit in the gallon bag. The children complete their readings and journals for literature groups outside of class as a standing assignment. They know that there is a reading and response assignment due every Monday, Wednesday, and Friday for class. When it comes time to work on their reading, the children look at their reading contracts to determine what chapters are required for the next group meeting. They read their assigned pages and upon completion respond in their journals or through some other semiotic system.

Literature groups meet every Monday, Wednesday, and Friday. Once the children have become engaged in writing workshop, I call the first reading group (by book title) to the carpet for our discussions. The children reading this book leave their writing workshop and come to our group meeting. They bring their bag of materials, and when we are finished sharing and all concerns have been addressed, the children return to their writing and the next group is called—again by book title. We continue through all groups (usually there are four to six books) in this manner. On these days, reading discussion groups take up the bulk of writing workshop time for me, and I cannot count on having many other interactions with the children other than brief conferences and continuous observation.

In the younger grades, kindergarten and first grade, I also use reading contracts and literature groups. The reading contracts of developing readers usually span a one week period and the groups tend to meet every day. Their reading journals are usually stapled books or are more like portfolios, which include individual pieces of paper and different response choices.

Much of my integration with the content areas is accomplished through the literature groups. Therefore, the children are predominately reading and responding to nonfictional materials or fictional materials that are related to our study. In the early grades, my literature sets tend to focus on the science curriculum. In grades three through six, my literature sets revolve around the social studies curriculum. Literature sets in the early grades almost always can be adapted to include the kindergarten and first grade social studies concepts too.

Towards the close of reading/writing workshop time, we gather our materials together and engage in a brief sharing period discussing what the students have written and what they are working on. As the children put their writing notebooks away, they select a couple of books and proceed to sit at their desks and read until lunchtime. Depending upon the day, this time ranges from five to twenty minutes.

Buddy Reading, D.E.A.R. (Drop Everything and Read), or SSR (Sustained Silent Reading), or SQUAT (Sustained Quiet Uninterrupted Author Time), or SQUIRT (Sustained Quiet Uninterrupted Reading Time), or Whatever You Call It I provide a daily opportunity for independent free-choice reading. The duration of this reading time varies depending upon the day. Some days we stop and read more than once. Reading is always a choice of something to do when other work is completed and the class is not ready to move on to another activity. Books are also brought to the cafeteria to read after lunch.

Focused Skill and Strategy Instruction Tuesdays and Thursdays during writing workshop time is my opportunity to purposely pull groups together and/or work with children one-on-one who demonstrate specific needs. Although I do this impromptu and frequently throughout the day, every day, I know that these two days allow time for more focused, planned instruction without too many interruptions.

During these direct instructional periods, I choose the material that we will be working with and I generate the area of focus—not the child. I select materials that are at the child's developmental reading level, either independent or instructional, depending upon my intent, and I focus upon an area I have observed that requires additional support. This time is when I would most likely employ materials like magnetic letters, white boards, and leveled books. We would read and write together and work on strategies responding to print. We would employ such techniques as cut up sentences, word families, and language experience activities. I would also use this time for assessment, such as running records or miscue analysis.[5]

After Lunch Everyday after lunch, we sit together and I read from our ongoing novel. Some of the children like to draw pictures of the story as I read. I want my children to be exposed to good literature, various authors and genre, and to be able to comprehend a story line over a period of time, respond to oral materials, increase their listening vocabularies, and model how reading sounds and makes sense.

Teacher read aloud is usually followed by math. Although I integrate math as much as possible throughout our curriculum, I still feel more comfortable at this point in my learning, keeping a separate math time for us to work on strategies, skills, and practice. I include as many manipulatives and real-life experiences as possible. And in the younger grades, I use many Math Their Way[6] activities, including the daily calendar.

Content Study After math, we focus on our remaining content of study. This is the time that I use to accomplish everything that is not part of my language arts or math curriculum. In the intermediate grades, it is always science and/or some additional focus on social studies. Using inquiry as a starting point, I choose a broad area of curricular study that I know we are required to examine closely, such as electricity. I generate possibilities, materials, and examples for exploration. After introducing and discussing the topic, the children choose a specific area of electricity they want to learn more about and are interested in pursuing. They research and present their findings to the class in whichever format best fits our research.

The children's research projects always receive two grades: one for content and one for convention. The convention grade is used as a language arts grade, not a science grade. The children can work on these projects during research time and throughout the day when finished with other work. They may utilize their writing workshop time drafting their research reports within reason and on a teacher approved basis. In some cases, this may be the only time and support a child has to accomplish their goals. I try to be as flexible as possible in my decisions without jeopardizing or compromising other criteria and procedures. It also gives students a real-life purpose for writing workshop. They need to create a project of some nature and at the very least, one that includes brainstorming, drafting, note taking, and decision making.

When I find that the content topics I need to cover are so varied that integrating them with any of my literature would be too forced or ridiculous, I usually decide to have two themes: one carried out in the morning and the other in the afternoon.

Day Is Done We close each day with a cleaning and organizing period, and then come to the carpet to show and share before buses are called to go home. We share items from home, stories we wrote or wish to read, or we talk about events important to our lives. A good day is usually had by all.

Now What?

In Chapter 1, we looked at the rationale for meeting individual needs. In Chapter 2, we deciphered all of the federal codes to understand our legal obligations. In Chapter 3, we looked at a review of the literature and acknowledged our own personal beliefs and philosophies concerning teaching and learning. This chapter discussed ways in which I commonly implement my beliefs into practice, and now it is time to become more specific.

In Chapter 5, I will introduce you to a child by the name of Karen. Karen was diagnosed with brain cancer at the age of seven and was a student in my fifth grade class. Through Karen we will look at establishing goals, assessing work samples, evaluating progress, and observing specific examples of classroom application that supported her learning.

Notes

1. Rhodes, L. K., and C. Dudley-Marling. 1988. *Readers and Writers With a Difference: A Holistic Approach to Teaching Struggling Readers.* Portsmouth, NH: Heinemann.

2. I use the term shared reading for our morning carpet activities for lack of a better term. Not everyone who refers to shared reading means reading a morning picture book and poem. The term shared reading is used frequently and takes on different connotations depending upon the context and intent.

3. Related by genre, theme, author, concept, and so on, and includes a choice of developmental levels.

4. Some teachers refer to this as giving a book talk.

5. Goodman, Y .M., D. J. Watson, and C. L. Burke. 1987. *Reading Miscue Inventory: Alternative Procedures.* NY: Richard C. Owen Publishers, Inc.

6. Baratta-Lorton, M. 1995. *Mathematics Their Way.* NY: Addison-Wesley Publishing Company.

5

Karen: A Portrait of a Special Needs Student

Karen

Karen is a ten-year-old girl in remission from brain cancer. Her tested ability indicates that she reads at a third-grade level and writes at a fourth-grade level. She is in the fifth grade. Based upon this information, your job is to create Karen's curriculum. What are your expectations or assumptions about her as a learner? Specifically:

- What does Karen look like to you as a learner?
- How do you think her handwriting will compare to the other children's? Her spelling?
- What are your thoughts regarding structuring her curriculum to accommodate her needs and accomplish her IEP goals?
- How do you need to adapt your curriculum?
- What does Karen need as a learner?
- How can you support her in the classroom?
- What reading material do we start with on Monday?

Karen's special education documents state that Karen is a student currently in remission from brain cancer. A three centimeter tumor was detected on her brain stem when she was in the second grade at the age of seven. It was removed and followed by massive treatments of radiation and chemotherapy. She has a 40 percent hearing loss in her left ear. This will be her first steady year of reentry to school. Her previous report cards reflect that prior to surgery Karen was performing as an "A" student in all subject areas and social behaviors.

She is now a fifth-grade student receiving special education services. Table 5-1 shows testing documentation from her special education folder.

Based upon this testing, Table 5-2 displays Karen's IEP goals that were established.

Brigance Reading Test	
Sight Vocabulary:	100% @ 3rd grade
	50% @ 4th grade
Reading Comprehension:	70% @ 3rd grade
Stanford Diagnostic Test	
Auditory Vocabulary	2.7 grade equivalent
Reading Comprehension	3.7 grade equivalent
Brigance Reading Test	
Spelling:	mid-3rd-grade level
Writing Sentences:	5th-grade level

Table 5-1. Testing

Reading:

Improve to a mid-fourth-grade level

Demonstrate reading test mastery @ 80% or better

Writing:

Improve to a fourth-grade level

Writing grades @ 80% or better

Spelling skills @ mid-third grade or better

Sentences edited with 80% accuracy

Capitalizations used with 80% accuracy

Punctuation with 80% accuracy

Table 5-2. Annual Goals

Halstead-Reitan Intermed Tests Category II T.P.T. (T Block)

Speech Perception II

Tapping

Lateral Preferences

Sensory Imperfection (errors)

Name Writing

Dynamotor

Grooved Pegboard

Trails

Seashore Rhythm test

PIAT-R

WISC-II

WRAML

Table 5-3. Neuropsychological Testing

Karen was being seen by a neuropsychologist. The neuropsychologist's report (Table 5-3) is included in Karen's records and is being used as substantiating documentation with regards to additional testing data and academic determinations.

It was stated by the neuropsychologist that,

"It was evident in this evaluation that Karen does not process language accurately. Although she was average for her age in spelling words to diction, she was severely impaired in her ability to select words correctly spelled from misspelled alternatives. When reading aloud, she either mispronounced words (e.g., 'ich' instead of 'its,' 'coset' instead of 'closet') or pronounced incorrect words (e.g., 'can' for 'cane,' 'tied' for tried.') Even on a relatively simple aphasia screening exam, Karen's difficulties with language were evident. Errors in articulation, reading, repetition, and spelling were noted. She was slow in performing both mental and written calculations. She was observed using finger and dot counting methods to obtain sums and differences that ordinarily are stored in memory as 'table knowledge.' The type of errors that Karen committed are indicative not only of an articulation disorder, but also of an underlying disturbance of general language processing."

Creating a Portrait of Karen

In summarizing the data:

- Karen is below grade level in reading and writing.
- She needs to improve her reading to a mid-fourth-grade level with 80 percent accuracy.
- She needs to improve her overall writing to a fourth-grade level with 80 percent mastery.

Based upon this information, what are our expectations or assumptions about Karen? How do we create a program to support her strengths and literacies. Where do we begin? This is usually where I run into a great deal of trouble. I am not a person that does very well with abstract concepts. In fact, I am a very visual and concrete person. I am having difficulty creating a composite sketch of a ten-year-old girl with brain cancer that performs a year below grade level in writing and two years below grade level in reading.

I do not get a picture of Karen as a learner. I do not see her or hear her voice. Any program I create now would be based upon insufficient evidence and information—not demonstrated need. I need more clues into her learning. I need to see her work samples. Informal data, such as authentic measures and field notes, are not generally considered official documentation. However, for this documentation we can turn to our class records and working portfolios.

Meet Karen

In Figure 5-1, Karen is eight years old undergoing cancer treatment and posing for the camera.

Background

An Interview with Karen's Mother, Sue Susan Maclure is a divorced mother of two daughters, Valerie age twelve and Karen age ten. Both children reside in the home with their mother. At the age of seven, Karen, then considered a perfectly healthy child, stepped out of their car to greet her grandmother and ran directly into her cement mailbox. She never saw it.

A doctor's examination revealed a three centimeter tumor located on Karen's brain stem. It was diagnosed as cancerous and Karen was not

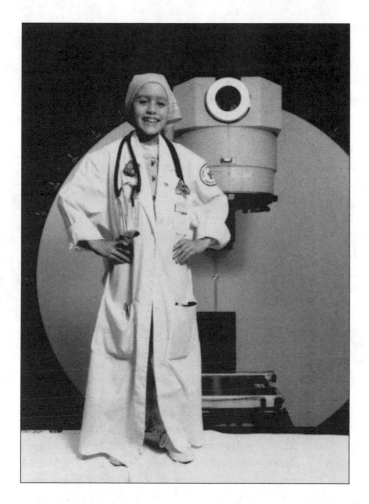

Figure 5-1. Karen

allowed to return home. She immediately underwent surgery followed by radical radiation and chemotherapy treatments. Karen was in the beginning of her second semester of second grade. She would not return that school year.

She returned to school in the fall as a third grader. Due to her continued treatments, she was sick quite frequently. She was also very weak and tired extremely easily. The radiation treatment had destroyed areas of her pituitary gland and Karen had stopped growing. She was still the size of a second grader and weighed only thirty-two pounds. Her first dose of chemotherapy left her with a 40 percent hearing loss in her left ear within two hours of injection. Her skin was jaundiced and she was bald. She wore a blue bandanna to school everyday, but many days it would be ripped off by her classmates and tossed around the playground like a Frisbee. Several times Karen had been locked and held captive in a bathroom stall while her classmates tormented her. Many days she would come to school only to leave early, exhausted or in tears. She was also falling behind her classmates academically and this disturbed her a great deal. Sue stated that there was a home tutor that had been provided early on, but she was considered gruff and on the border of being downright mean. Karen was disturbed by her and the relationship soon ended.

Toward the middle of fourth grade, Karen began a more steady reentry to school. Her medical treatments were almost completed and she was getting her strength back. By the spring of that year, it was determined that Karen was failing the fourth grade. Sue had two choices: retain Karen as a fourth grader, or place Karen in special education classes and receive support from the learning disabilities resource teacher, speech therapist, and a district hearing specialist. Her medical history automatically qualified her for special education resources. Since Karen did not want to be retained, Sue agreed, and Karen began receiving services on a pull-out basis. Fifth grade was to be her first full year of reentry to the public school. She had spent the summer working with her psychologist preparing her emotionally for the event.

What I Found After reviewing Karen's records I discovered some interesting information. The first was that Karen had missed approximately two hundred and thirty-two days of school between the middle of second grade and the end of fourth grade.[1] Her poor performance in school may have been related more to her absences then an assumed disability as a result of the cancer, surgery, and/or treatments. It seemed likely that any child receiving 50 percent less of an education would certainly be expected to perform below the average of their peers. This was an important distinction. This could mean that Karen's medical problems may not have been the sole cause or primary factor for her tested performance as suspected. It could have been an attendance issue. Coupled with the fact that she now had a 40 percent hearing loss and was not receiving in-class support for her work or during her testing, it opened additional possibilities. The statement, "*This may not be the best Karen can do because she has cancer,*" may be questionable. It may just be that with additional support and added time we could help her achieve the same level as her peers and return her to a normal academic life. Very few children survive Karen's type of brain cancer. Many do not live through the treatment or reach remission. The doctors have no idea what to expect, nor do they know how her capabilities may have been affected—short term or long term.[2]

There are also discrepancies in her testing data and IEP. When we look back at the testing we see that on the Brigance Writing Test she scored at a fifth-grade level for writing sentences. Her IEP goal for writing is recorded as needing to improve to a fourth-grade level with 80 percent mastery. This will need to be investigated further.

Looking at Karen's Writing Performance

Morning Journal In class, Karen writes each morning in her daily journal. Although the children have the option of free writing, I usually provide a prompt for children who wish to have a more directed format. Karen's journal writings reflect responses to prompts; typically they are one to two sentences in length. She does not appear to be generating or creating new knowledge.[3] She writes:

Journal Entry Dated: 8/27

Prompt: What are your goals for this school year?

My goals are to go to school and to learn math, Science, Salshol Studies, Reading, and wrighting!

Journal Entry Dated: 9/13

Prompt: Would you like to live until the age of 100? Why?

Yes I would like to live in till I am a hundred years old because I would like a very long and happy life. And because it is kind of famace to be one hundred years old.

Although Karen's journal responses are brief, there is a sense of voice. I can get an idea of who Karen is as a person. She is honest and vulnerable about her desire to be famous. In one entry, she expresses anger over her friend's relocation to Utah:

Prompt: What is the nicest thing your friend has ever done? The meanest?

The nices thing my friend has done was come to my birthday party and the meanest thing she did was move to Utah!

From Karen's writings I can tell that she recognizes the main function of print, which is to communicate and express ideas. In her journal, she uses print to communicate her feelings, desires, and concerns.

Karen's journal responses employ a writing strategy that children generally don't utilize in their responses unless they have had some initial modeling, exposure, or direction. Typical student responses to the same prompts in August and September generally tend to look more like this:

Prompt: Charlotte was happy with the book's ending. How did you feel? Why?

Yes, I liked it too

Prompt: What are your goals for the school year?

Bring up my grades

But Karen rewords the question in her answers. In this manner, the reader knows what Karen is responding to. You'll notice that Karen's writing is more developed in sentence structure then these shorter examples. Karen tends to write in complete thoughts and sentences. She appears to utilize punctuation and capitalization consistently and conventionally (expectant for her age and grade), and has a good sense of the use of commas for separating a list of objects in print.

Her spelling is either conventional and/or represents a good sense of phonemes. This is an interesting fact given her 40 percent hearing loss. When spelling, children often write the sounds in words that they hear. Karen's use of convention is very good considering she has not really had consistent instruction since the second grade, two and a half years ago. Her hearing loss also attributes to some mispronunciations in her speech. In many cases, when a word is misspelled, the first thing I ask Karen or any child to do is to pronounce the word for me. Many times the child is merely pronouncing the word incorrectly. We can be very sloppy talkers in this country. At times, we do not articulate very well. For a child with a hearing loss who reads lips, I'm sure it creates some hurdles as well as inaccurate assumptions of ability.

It's also interesting to note that even though she misspelled the word *wrighting*, she knew that the phoneme *ight* made the same sound as *ite*. I would eventually like for Karen to work towards expanding her journal responses to include more information and detail. My immediate goal is for Karen to start generating her own topics. I want her to feel comfortable responding to and valuing her creations and thinking. This would confirm that Karen is seeing herself as a writer. She would be demonstrating risk taking and trust in the curriculum, herself, and our classroom community. Autonomy is the goal.

Writing Workshop In writing workshop, Karen initially does not like to write a lot. She says that her arm gets tired and she doesn't know what to say. Her first two days of writing workshop time are mostly spent copying poems and illustrations of Shel Silverstein. Her first attempts at free writing resemble the genre of a journal response. In this next entry, we see that she is writing about something familiar. She appears to be writing an answer to a question she or somebody else created.

> *Writing Workshop Entry Dated: 8/23*
>
> *Possible Prompt: What is your favorite food?*
>
> *My favorite food's are chicken rice soup, chines* food, & Lucky wish bone. I like these foods because there taste, and because Smell good, and cause I like shrimp, chicken fingers garlek* Bread, & fries. I also like rice, beef chowman* & because I like chicken.*

In her entry, she circles the words she believes are misspelled.[4] She circles three out of four misspellings, not catching the homonym *there*. Her remaining misspellings are phonetic. I notice there are two words capitalized in the middle of sentences that should not be (*Bread, Smell*). She is applying the capitalization of proper nouns, but not consistently. Her sentences look conventional with regard to beginning capitalization and ending punctuation. She is consistently using commas to separate strings of words. In the word *food's*, Karen is demonstrating the use of apostrophes with possessives. In this example she is overgeneralizing the use of the rule and applying it towards plurals. We can work on this skill if it continues and remains consistent.

During the writing of her second entry, I notice Karen using her crayons to aid her in her writing and her spelling. This is a good strategy. She is copying the words from the crayon wrappers as she writes:

> *Writing Workshop Entry Dated: 8/24*
>
> *My favorite colors are jungle green, cerulean, red, purple because they are pretty, and colorfull! I also have mor favorite colors. They are wild watermelon, hot magenta, shocking pink, razzle dazzle rose, radicalred, vivid tangerine, atomic tangerine, mellow yellow, sun glow, laser lemon, outrageous[†] orange and last neon carrot! I like these colors because they are very bright colors.*

[†] In Karen's original journal the word *outrageous* falls at the end of a line and cannot be completed. She hyphenates the word conventionally (out-) and moves onto the next line.

In this second attempt at self-generated writing, Karen again demonstrates consistency with convention in capitalization, spelling, and punctuation. We also see that her entry includes an obvious beginning, middle, and end. She starts her piece with a topic sentence and ends with a closing that summarizes the reasons she likes all of the colors. We also see that she is using exclamation points on the colors that she truly likes the best. She hyphenates the word *outrageous* correctly and again demonstrates an overgeneralization of the use of apostrophes in possessives.

Upon completing the previous entry, Karen immediately began another writing piece. This writing draft took on the shape of a creative story. She shared it in the author's chair and was our first author to share that year. This was her draft:

Writing Workshop Draft Dated: 8/24

The Nosy Pig let

There once lived a pig that was so nosy he did't have anytime to do anything else. when he did his math he was done at the same time because he saw all of the answers. at reading time he wanted to read after his friends. his name is Charlie. But people call him nosy! He is sad sometimes because people don't relly like him even no they pretend to. His friend's pretend to like him to! One day a girl named Sue was skating she fell down and hert her leg she couldn't get up. There was nobody around when she fell. Good thing Charlie was walking to school. Charlie found her laying on the ground. He picked Sue up he took her to his house and told his parents and he called the hospitle. The hospitle took good care of her! They found that she broke her leg, and sprang her rist. After every body found out what he did! Every body thanked him! The parent's thanked him to. Every body was Charlie's friend now, But Sue was Charlie's best friend.

The

End

I am pleased to see that this piece appears to look more like a creative narrative than her previous entries. I am not sure of what supplied the scaffold for this topic, but there are obvious signs of Karen in the text. The main character is shunned by his friends. The piglet is not liked, and is not comfortable with his school work. Karen explains that the pig feels sad because of this. She goes on to state how some people pretend they are your friends when they really aren't. At the close of this last statement, she chooses to end with an exclamation point. She decides to resolve the piglet's conflict with the introduction of a secondary character, Sue. Sue helps Karen solve her problem. Sue's accident allows the piglet an opportunity to show everybody that he is a likeable, caring, good little pig. When people find that out, they begin to like him. It introduces the hospital as a setting, and a place that takes good care of people. She summarizes the story with a closing statement: But Sue was his best friend.

Her story reflects that Karen is internalizing print by relating it to her own life and using her life experiences as a framework for transacting and interacting with print. She is internalizing writing, learning to manipulate it, and making it her own. She's transferring knowledge and making connections. Technically, her story is very cohesive and correctly follows the beginning, middle, and end format. She demonstrates the ability to recognize and write causal relationships when she speaks of feeling sad because the children do not like the pig. She also uses a conflict/resolution format as the platform for her plot and story development. She introduces characters, setting, and details.

Her sentences are predominately conventional with regard to capitalization and punctuation. There are a couple of sentences that drop the initial capital letter, but I tend to believe that this is due to the fact that this is a working draft from her notebook and not a completed piece meant to be seen. She demonstrates the use of capital letters at the beginning of sentences in almost all of her work as well as here in this text. I am not concerned about this. In future revisions, I would expect that Karen will fix the capitalizations without guidance. Some of her sentences are run-on sentences and could be separated into two sentences, but all are complete thoughts.

Her spelling is predominately conventional and the rest is phonetic. She capitalizes proper nouns and demonstrates a good sense of commas. She uses two contractions: *didn't* and *don't*. In both words, she removes the correct letter (the vowel) and demonstrates proper placement of the apostrophe. I am not sure if her spelling of *did't* is a mistake in writing or if she assumes it to be correct. She spells the contraction *don't* correctly, so this is an area to investigate further. I am also curious as to her thinking behind the spelling of *pig let*. I don't notice that she misspells any other words because of syllable breaks when she writes, so I am unsure as to whether this is a writing style to create atmosphere towards the pig, or if she has a misconception about the word. It could just be her personality, or she could be playing with print.

I notice that she is overgeneralizing the use of possessive apostrophes in this piece also. She consistently separates the word *every body* and uses the homonym *to* in incorrect context. The words *hospitle*, *sprang*, and *rist*, can be worked on and corrected. The incorrect spelling of *sprang* and *rist* may be the result of a hearing/pronunciation issue. The word *hospitle* is a word I suspect we will see many times in Karen's writing. Therefore, it is a good word to work on for convention. This would be a good time to review some words from her readings that have *le, al, ol, el,* and *ul* endings, which all sound similar. This knowledge will make her feel more comfortable with her risk taking. Karen is a perfectionist. She doesn't like making mistakes. In fact, mistakes scare Karen. If I make a mistake, I assume it's because I messed up. If Karen makes a mistake, she thinks she either has another brain tumor or there is something wrong with her brain because of the cancer. Karen doesn't *just* make mistakes. It's not that simple. Knowing that there are many variations for the same sound in our language will help her take more chances and lighten up on herself a little bit.

We have some solid, workable information concerning Karen here. We are seeing growth and patterns in her learning. We have some great starting places for dialogue and interaction with Karen about this text. We have identified areas to keep an eye on and monitor. Instructionally, we need to see if these areas take care of themselves. If they look as if they may be developing into a pattern or remain consistent, then these areas will need to be addressed as mini-lessons or conferences with Karen. Right now, praise is in order. We can address other issues tomorrow.

During this time in the classroom, we were also working on writing our family stories or *his*tories as we called them. We continually generate family *his*tories throughout the year as one of our class objectives. Our first writing piece and exercise for this project was to create a Snapshot Story. In my journal I wrote about Karen:

> She finished her Snapshot Story, so she said she was going to record a new story on the WW [writing workshop] status check. At end of WW she asked if she could share. She had written a new story based on Jon Scieszka's book The True Story of the Three Little Pigs.[6] She shared after lunch. She was mentally revising as she read. She made pencil notations when she sat down to read and again while she was reading. She also read the story to Mrs. Sheraton (her hearing specialist) after school. Mrs. Sheraton mentioned that K got a pencil out and made revisions as she read it to her.

This is the draft that Karen shared:

> The three pigs and the fox who lived across the street.
>
> Once upon a time there live three pigs. And the three pigs hated foxes. And thats how the whole thing happen. A cross the street live four pigs. There house was getting to small so they had to move. The three little pigs where sad because they where there best friends. But once they found out there was some

body else moving in. The three pigs where excited, and cureuse who was moving in. A cuple of weeks late the person wouldn't come out. So the three pigs went over to the house to see how moved in. It was a fox. But the three pigs didn't now that. When they nocked on the door the door opened slowly. The three pigs found out the person who moved in was a fox. But the three pigs weren't sckared of the fox. The fox said can I help you. Yes we just wanted to see who lived here because you have not come out yet, and we were cureuse who moved in. The three pigs wheren't scared of the fox because he is kind, and nicer then every other fox. Would you like to come in yes. Thank you! But first tell me your name. The fox said my name is Jonithin. What is yours. Well my name is albert, mines Alex, mines erik. And then the three pigs, and the fox lived happily ever after.

Karen includes one of Scieszka's sentences from the book in her own story: *And that's how the whole thing happen[ed]*. She is writing in a fairy tale genre. The story begins with *Once upon a time* and concludes with *[they] lived happily ever after*. Her spelling in this first draft is either conventional or phonetic. All of her sentences begin with capital letters and she demonstrates control over appropriate sentence structure. Her story has a beginning, a middle, and an end. She uses dialogue in her story, which I have not seen in her previous work. There is no evidence that she is attempting to implement quotation marks. As Karen's writing becomes more complex, she will eventually be exposed to all kinds of punctuation.

Two circumstances should be noted of Karen while she revised her draft as she read. She mentally revised and self-corrected the text when she shared in the author's chair. She also shared her story with Mrs. Sheraton and kept a pencil in her hand. She revised in writing as she read. This not only demonstrates that she revises text as needed, but that she is monitoring her comprehension and self-correcting as she reads. In the social context of our whole language classroom, Karen stumbles upon an immediate need to implement her education and employs stages of the writing process. She wants to make her message clear to her audience. Revision becomes a problem solving strategy for constructing meaning. Karen demonstrates that she can manipulate stages of the writing process to accommodate her need.

Looking at Karen's Reading

Literature Discussion Groups In literature discussion group, Karen is reading the novel *Maniac Magee* by Jerry Spinelli.[7] The following excerpts are from her first reading journal entries dated in September:

Reading Journal Responses: Excerpts/Maniac Magee

- *I would most want to be Maniac Magee because I would like to be able to get a big knot out, and because I would like to read as good as him because I like reading.*

- *I think this story is sad because Maniac's parents died on a trolly that crashed on a bridge, and Grayson was getting to be a good friend to Maniac Magee and died.*

- *If my character could be an animal it would be a cheata because he can run fast and because he likes to run.*

The journal responses to Karen's first literature book, *Maniac Magee*, show that Karen comprehends the text and is able to infer and discuss the author's meaning with significance to her and her life. She carries with her the elements of the plot, main idea, sequence, causal relationships, conflicts, and relationships between characters, throughout the duration of this novel.

Her written responses also reflect inference level application. I want to point out that the brevity in Karen's answers should never be mistaken as a lack of knowledge, effort, or limited comprehension. This is a child who, literally, has had a small portion of her brain removed followed by massive dosages of radiation and chemotherapy. The doctors don't know the effects of any of these treatments on Karen or her life. Based upon Karen's comments, her medical records, and her demonstrated behaviors, her fluctuating loss of memory began after her illness and is of much frustration and disruption to Karen's life and performance. Karen's answers usually are brief because she doesn't really like to write her responses; and because it is still not comfortable for her to casually respond in writing. It takes time and concentration. She first needs to come up with an idea for a response based upon her reading. She then needs to understand what she has read, find some element of the text she wishes to share, and be able to transfer these thoughts into writing—using her best convention possible. That's a lot of work.

Karen demonstrates that her comprehension of this novel goes beyond a literal interpretation of the text, and that she extends interpretations of the text to other situations and experiences. She appears to be gaining insight into herself through books. She is thinking about literature, constructing her own personal meanings, and sharing her constructions in a social arena with her peers. She reflects that she enjoys reading, and she demonstrates that she is able to ascertain the tone or mood from a novel.

Her behaviors reveal the importance of belonging to the class community and the reading groups. We know that learning is social and that all learning takes place in a social context. Karen respects the nature of the reading groups and values her participation in them. Because Karen is a quiet child by nature, I am not concerned with her reserved participation while she learns the format and becomes comfortable with the other children. Based upon her journal responses, I don't believe that her lack of participation reflects a concern for her comprehension at this point.

In one of the following journal entries, her comments regarding the term "pepper," a baseball term, confirms the fact that Karen uses intertextuality, meaning that she connects the story to other texts and turns to text to verify or clarify ideas.

In my professional journal I noted:

- *K sat quietly and listened to everybody discuss the book. When asked about what she thought about Maniac, she responded by reading her journal response, which talked about why she would like to be Maniac. She read it word for word with no added conversation. Nor did she join in the other conversations. The children began sharing their journal entries around the circle. Because she had shared her entry previously, we skipped over her to the next member of the group and she said, "Hey, you skipped me!" I apologized and explained our wrong assumptions and asked her to proceed. She reread exactly how and what she read five minutes previously and stated that although it was the same, it was still her turn to share.*

- *In reading group Karen has been sharing her journal entries. She laughs with the other children, but has yet to participate further in the discussions. Karen said that she should have known what the term pepper meant in the Frank & Ernest book[8] because it was also in Maniac Magee. She then found the location of the word in both books for me.*

- *She is still not talking much in group, but today she led the group.*

Independent Reading While Karen was reading *Maniac Magee*, she was also independently reading the book *Charlotte's Web*.[9] She chose to write her responses to this book as well. I unexpectedly found the following excerpt in Karen's journal.

Charlotte's Web — September

One reason why the book was sad was because Fern's father was going to kill Wilbur with an axe because he was too little. Another reason is because Charlotte died. Charlotte and Wilbur were real good friends. It was sad when she died. That is how I would feel. I liked Charlotte. Charlotte could sew all the names into her web and she was nice. She said nice things and she helped Wilbur by making him famous and making words in the spider web. Another sad part is she died before seeing her babies. Wilbur was sad because nobody wanted to play with him.

In her entry, she demonstrates the ability to identify, follow, and explore the relationships between characters. She uses information from the book to form opinions and cites examples to support her comments. It appears that in her discussion of Wilbur nearly being murdered by Fern's father that she identifies cause and effect relationships. Her comprehension of the story is reflected in her empathy and fondness for Charlotte. Karen also discusses the story in terms of her own emotions, which is a true sign that she interacts with and relates to print. The format of her entry, its sentence structure, capitalization, punctuation, and spellings are conventional.

In my personal journal I wrote:

- *K came in this morning and said that she read all of Charlotte's Web. She had journal questions done and dated according to an old contract. Journal questions were short. Today after school we worked on thoroughly answering journal questions and rewrote one of hers. Her retelling of parts was very good. We discussed how to improve the answer by adding more details from the book. K condensed the whole concept by saying, "Oh — I need to make it longer." We then looked for a new book. I selected a couple and asked her to see if she wanted to read one of them. She said, "Let me see" and began reading the first page. When I asked her what she thought, she informed me that she was not done yet. The page she was reading turned out to be an author's introduction page to the story and she said, "Oh, I hate that! It takes too long. Why don't they just get to the story?" And she then began to read page one. She took the books home with her to decide.*

Reading Skills In August, the media specialist required all of the children to complete library skills, which included locating information from the card catalog, alphabetizing forty words, and using guide words. My journal entry noted:

- *The media specialist had the kids perform library skills. One paper asked the children to alphabetize words (about 40) and to state silent letters in words by looking them up in the dictionary. Karen alphabetized them quickly. She never bothered to look them up in the dictionary for silent sounds. She said the word to me and matter-of-factly stated the silent letter. When I told her she could look them up, she stated that this was easy 'Listen... kite - e, night - g, knife - k...*

Establishing Goals and Criteria

Based on the sampling of work and information provided previously, let's review and begin to answer the questions about Karen stated at the beginning of the chapter.

- What does Karen look like to you as a learner?
- How do you think her handwriting will compare to the other children's? Her spelling?
- What are your thoughts regarding structuring her curriculum to accommodate her needs and accomplish her IEP goals?
- How do you need to adapt your curriculum?
- What does Karen need as a learner?
- How can you support her in the classroom?
- What reading material do we start with on Monday?

Through Karen's informal data I am able to get a better picture of who she is as a learner and as a person. I am also able to gain a better understanding of how I need to plan for my classroom and the different structures that will need to be created to support the flexibility of our curriculum.

In order to do the planning for both Karen and my class, I need to know how to transfer my ideas of literacy into the curriculum. What is it that I want all of my children to do, demonstrate, and/or accomplish through our curriculum this school year? What *does* learning look like in my classroom? What do I *want* the learning to look like in my classroom? What are the elements of literacy in a holistic program? What does an independent reader look like? What are the observable strengths of a *good* reader and writer? These are all questions that enter my mind as I prepare a program or a lesson.

It's difficult to write a program or assess a person's strengths in that program if we don't know what we're looking for or what literacy and learning looks like. What specific elements and behaviors do you want to see demonstrated in your classroom? What does a strong, print-rich curriculum look like to you? As you begin to write your ideas down, your list can become a guideline for you in your planning. You can use it to remind yourself of what you are looking for in your program. It can be used as your own checklist of benchmark behaviors or criteria. As you observe these behaviors for each student, you can mark them. This list will serve as a planner for future focus lessons with the child as well as allow you to keep abreast of where each child is in their learning. It will assist you immensely when it comes time for conferences and report cards, and it will allow you to speak more knowledgeably and specifically about the child.

What is it that you are looking for in your program? What criteria, goals, behaviors, and expectations would you like to establish for all of the students in your classroom? The following lists contain my goals for each child in my language arts program—they drive my program.

Reading Goals

1. Constructs meaning
2. Skims
3. Highlights difficult words
4. Makes notes, diagrams
5. Turns to text to verify and clarify ideas
6. Connects story to personal experience
7. Connects story to others in group
8. Connects story to other texts
9. Asks for clarification
10. Revises/extends interpretations
11. Helps others think through questions
12. Uses text for confirmation, exploration
13. Initiates literature discussions
14. Considers differences of opinion
15. Shares thinking with others
16. Selects books independently
17. Samples a variety of genres
18. Chooses books of appropriate difficulty
19. Reads silently for sustained periods
20. Shows pleasure in reading
21. Makes predictions about text
22. Uses prior knowledge
23. Rereads for meaning
24. Uses picture clues

25. Uses context for identifying unfamiliar words
26. Reads for a variety of purposes
27. Retells
28. Summarizes
29. Discusses personal understanding of main idea
30. Understands sequencing
31. Understands cause and effect
32. Understands fact and opinion
33. Understands reality from fantasy
34. Understands text that utilizes elements of flashback
35. Understand texts that utilizes dialects
36. Revises interpretations after discussions
37. Self-corrects
38. Sustains comprehension throughout a chapter book
39. Uses phonetic clues
40. Learns, understands, and employs new vocabulary
41. Follows plot and sees relationships between characters
42. Reads orally with fluency
43. Reads orally with expression
44. Engages in discussions that go beyond literal understanding of the text
45. Employs the process of inferring
46. Identifies setting
47. Identifies characters
48. Discusses tone or mood of the book
49. Discusses various authors' works
50. Chooses to read

Writing Goals

1. Chooses and develops a topic
2. Shows awareness of audience
3. Uses a variety of textual cues, such as charts, subheadings, graphs

4. Shares writing
5. Demonstrates growth in story length
6. Revises, edits, and rewrites
7. Publishes writing
8. Creates stories that have a beginning, a middle, and an end
9. Uses correct punctuation
10. Responds appropriately to others' writing
11. Forms letters conventionally
12. Writes neatly
13. Uses reference sources
14. Brainstorms or uses prewriting strategies
15. Moves from invented to conventional spellings
16. Chooses to write
17. Spaces letters and words appropriately
18. Employs the use of indenting paragraphs
19. Employs quotation marks
20. Demonstrates cohesive writing
21. Experiments with genres
22. Uses age-appropriate vocabulary
23. Uses age-appropriate sentence structure

Speaking Goals

1. Volunteers to speak and share in front of others
2. Practices prior to presentations
3. Speaks clearly and loudly
4. Makes eye contact
5. Explains ideas clearly

Listening Goals

1. Listens attentively to class discussions
2. Demonstrates the ability to comprehend and carry out oral instructions

General Goals:

1. Cooperates with others
2. Contributes to group work
3. Learns from watching others
4. Generates solutions and ideas to solve problems
5. Plans, organizes, and carries out tasks
6. Accepts responsibility as a member of our classroom community

Documenting Karen's Growth Over Time

Writing Throughout the school year Karen published over twenty-five books and at least twenty poems. She generated the following types of writing: news articles, research reports, creative stories, factual stories, journal entries, essays, charts, banners, posters, signs, cards, recipes, illustrations, art work, notes, memos, letters, maps, diagrams, cartoons, and timelines. She utilized writing for record keeping, organizing, enjoyment, communication, planning, documenting, expressing her thoughts and feelings, sharing/socializing, note taking, and understanding and clarifying concepts.

Karen never received a writing grade below a B (or 80 percent) during the 1993–94 school year. Her writing grades were based upon convention as well as content. She completed the school year with straight As.

For purposes of establishing a grade level in both writing and spelling, I consulted the district's curriculum guidelines. Karen's overall work samples met or surpassed all districtwide fifth-grade criteria with the exception of writing a business letter, which I did not teach that school year. In fact, except for the business letter, she also exceeded the district's criteria for sixth-grade writing as well. Spelling criteria, addressed in the district's guidelines under the writing objectives, stated that Karen needed to employ a variety of spelling and demonstrate the ability to use a dictionary and a thesaurus. Karen did demonstrate these competencies in the classroom and in the library. In addition, Karen did demonstrate that she was consistently moving toward conventional spellings in her writing. There was little difference in quantity or quality between Karen's spelling inventions and the other children's inventions. In actuality, Karen had less inventions than most of the children because she used the dictionary so frequently.

With regard to my whole language criteria for writing and Karen's demonstrated competencies, she successfully completed all of the writing criteria established for fifth-grade students except for "indents paragraphs." However, I did not work independently with Karen on indenting paragraphs in any of our conferences.

To view Karen's growth throughout the school year, I assessed her first and last writing workshop entries of the year. Her first piece was the August entry regarding her favorite foods. For a forty-seven word text, 89 percent of the spellings were conventional. There were two capitalizations of common nouns and two proper nouns not capitalized. There was also a plural written as a possessive.

The following is Karen's last writing workshop entry.

May 2, 94 **draft**

Once upon a time lived three pigs, a fox, and a rabbit. The rabbit's name is Bugs Bunny. The foxe's name is Wilbur and the pig's names are Robert, Jon, and Dan. Bugs Bunny was a crazy bunny! He messed around with the fox. So Wilbur gave up. Finally Bugs said, let's go for a walk. It's good exersize! They went for a walk and Bugs Bunny and Wilbur became good friends! A few blocks more they walked and came upon the first pig Robert. The fox said let's get out of here before I start sneezing and blow the poor pig's house down. Bugs Bunny said now come on wait a minute! I want to talk to him. Bugs said little pig little pig come out its just Bugs Bunny. Do you have anybody else with you? Ya my friend Wilbur. Wilbur I hate foxes! Im getting out of here. Wilbur get that pig to come talk to me. You tell him you are a nice fox and you've learned your lesson! Little pig little pig I am a nice fox now and learned a very big lesson. There was no answer! Bugs said blow the house down! So I could talk to him. Well ok! So he huffed and he puffed and blew the little pigs house down that was made of sticks. He was gone. All that was left was sticks. So they walked on. The next house they came upon was Jon the secent little pig but a little bite older and stupider. His house was made of straw and can you guess what? robert the first pig was there! Bugs Bunny said little pigs little pigs please come out, me and my friend won't hurt you! not by the prickleys of our chiny chin chins. Wilbur tell them we won't hurt them and you've learned your lesson. OK. Well OK! Little pigs little pigs let us come in by your prickly, prickley hairs we won't hurt you and I've learned a very good lesson. There wasn't any answer. Blow em down said Bugs. So the fox huffed and puffed and blew out the hairs of the second brothers house made out of straws. Nothing was there but straws and prickles of hair. So they walked on. They came to the theird and last pig of all Dan. I remember this guy. He was made of brains and got me in big trouble. Little pigs, little pigs come out and talk to us. We won't hurt you! Don't listen to them. Tell them to come out and talk to us we won't hurt them and you've learned a very

very good lesson. Ok. Ok one more time. Little pigs little pigs please come out we won't hurt you and I have learned a very very very good lesson. Please come out and talk to us or I'll blow your house in. Don't listen to him you can't blow a house built of bricks down! But suddenly the pigs heard huffing and puffing. They started laughing! The fox gave up. It's no use Bugs. I can't blow a house with bricks down. Oh, yes you can. Try one more time ok. Ok. So he huffed and he puffed and guess what? Oh my god I did it!"

(P.S. Heres a secret. The rabbit really blew up the house made of bricks. (I don't think anybody could.) The main thing about the story is Bugs Bunny was bossing Wilbur around and he finaly did something to help. The other main thing of the story is they wanted to talk to one of the pigs)

Karen's illustrations of her story show a rabbit pouring gasoline and fire onto the brick house, and the rabbit and fox saying, "Will you talk to us?" Her cover features pictures of all the characters.

Karen's story is 620 words in length. Seven of these words (or .1 percent) are not spelled according to convention. Three of the inventions are contractions that are spelled correctly, but are missing their apostrophe marks. Another word "secent" is spelled conventionally later on in the text. The remaining invented words are "bite" for bit, "finaly," and "theird." Table 5-4 reflects Karen's growth in writing.

Karen shows that she can choose and develop a topic, write for an audience, move from invented to conventional spellings, set a tone or mood for her writing, and use other printed works for story ideas. She has shown growth in story length and development. Her sentence structure and vocabulary are age appropriate and all of her sentences and proper nouns begin with capital letters.

	August	*May*
Number of words	47	620
Inventions	11%	0.10%
Surface features	11%	0%
Use of voice	no	yes
Story contains plot	no	yes
Story is developed	no	yes

Table 5-4. Karen's Growth in Writing

Her punctuation is correct. Her story is cohesive and she is consistent in tense. Her story contains a beginning, a middle, and an end. She is writing in fairy-tale genre. She has utilized fairy-tale vocabulary and repeated text. But more importantly, Karen considers herself a writer.

Reading Based upon the literature read and the quality of Karen's responses to the texts, Karen has demonstrated that she is reading quality, age-appropriate literature, which places her nicely at or above her current grade level. Her class work with regard to literature discussions, journal responses, reading projects, and reading tests have surpassed the 80 percent criteria level established by her IEP. Karen completed the school year on the principal's list. She received straight As. She also mastered both the district and state assessment tests in reading. Both of these assessments establish mastery at 80 percent. Karen easily accomplished and surpassed her special education criteria.

Karen's work samples, my anecdotal records, and formal measures provided the documentation and evidence to substantiate that Karen met all of the objectives on my reading goals list for that school year. Our classroom format allowed for many opportunities in which Karen could engage in reading on a daily basis. She always chose to read and participate. She demonstrated that she read for a variety of purposes including:

- enjoyment
- socialization/inclusion
- to locate and retrieve information
- to learn
- to share and discuss
- to gather ideas for writing
- to provide structures for writing

Karen demonstrated growth throughout the school year in her reading experiences. The difficulty of the books she chose increased as did the quality of her journal responses. Karen began the school year with very little experience with complete texts. Prior to fifth grade, Karen was predominately reading short stories and excerpts from a basal reading series. She had little experience with reading novels. Novels differ from short stories in that they expose the reader to more of a variety of textual elements.

When reading a novel, the reader needs to sustain comprehension throughout an extended period of time. Plots and characters are more richly and intricately developed. Cause and effect scenarios are usually more prevalent and more difficult to detect because they are submerged in the context of the story. Elements of setting are more numerous and detailed.

Basal stories employ controlled vocabulary and sentence structures that are unnatural to our oral language and often appear and sound awkward. In this regard, basal readers actually made the reading task more difficult for Karen.

She began the school year reading *The Knights of the Kitchen Table*[10] as our first whole group modeling project. This book is directed toward children ages eight through ten. Karen ended the school year reading *The True Confessions of Charlotte Doyle*[11]; a book targeted for young adults ages nine through fourteen. The books she read increased in both difficulty and length. *The Knights of the Kitchen Table* contains fifty-five pages of text with at least one third of the text used for illustrations. *The True Confessions of Charlotte Doyle* is 232 pages of text. There is only one illustration included in an appendix. The illustration is a detailed, labeled drawing of the ship Charlotte sailed on.

Many of the books Karen read pertained to the Colonial and Revolutionary War periods. These books utilized British dialects and vocabulary, Native American dialects, rural Black dialects, colonial dialects and vocabulary, various archaic country dialects, and German and French language and vocabulary. The language and syntax of the stories were sometimes complex and unusual to the children's ears. The settings of the books were predominately unfamiliar to most of the students. Several of the books were set on sailing vessels. These texts were abundant with nautical terminology. Many of the books were set in the eastern part of the United States; unfamiliar to many of the children who reside in the desert. All of these textual features were handled nicely by Karen. They did not impede her efforts to understand meaning.

In her literature group setting, Karen read fairy tales, historical fiction, historical nonfiction, picture books, poems, charts, diagrams, biographies, maps, glossaries, novels, songs, and diaries. Her responses to *The Knights of the Kitchen Table* were illustrations she copied directly from the text. By the end of the school year, Karen was generating her own literature discussion questions for both herself and her group members. Her responses to literature increased in length and quality.

Karen shared her responses in literature group with her peers. During her first group sharing, I observed that Karen was very quiet and reserved. She did not respond to any group members when they shared, nor did she orally participate in the literature discussion of the book. She sat and listened, sharing only when she was called upon. By the end of the year, Karen had many experiences as group leader. She generated journal responses and initiated literature group discussions—often spontaneously outside of literature circle. She shared eagerly and demonstrated her ability to discuss literature and various literature genres.

Karen responded to the literature in numerous ways. She dressed as characters and made lists and glossaries of the characters detailing their relevance to the story line. She compared characters from one text to another and discussed how characters from one book would react to situations in a different book. Karen used art to create dioramas, murals, models, artifacts, book covers, and scenery. She drew settings, characters, and scenes from the stories. She created treasure boxes containing personal artifacts of literary characters.

Karen demonstrated various reading strategies throughout the year. When we began the school year, Karen's sole verbalization strategy for figuring out unknown words was to look them up in the dictionary. Karen now consciously employs strategies of reading ahead, looking for contextual clues, rereading, sounding out letters, asking somebody, skipping the words, or looking in the dictionary. She has also demonstrated an ability to transfer these strategies to other reading situations: predominately her expository reading of textbooks. Karen monitors her reading. This is evidenced by her self-correcting, predicting and confirming text, and documenting unknown vocabulary words and character glossaries.

Evidence of growth is further documented through a comparison of her Reading Miscue Inventories, shown in Table 5-5. Karen's miscue analysis indicates that she increased her reading comprehension or meaning construction on these measures from 73 percent to 80 percent between October and April. This percentile reflects Karen's ability to create meaning from the text. It represents how well Karen understands the story. Her grammatical relations strength percentage increased from 50 percent to 76 percent. This percentile shows that Karen is using the syntactic system well and her miscues result in acceptable grammatical structures. What she reads sounds like language.

Karen's overcorrections dropped from 10 percent to 4 percent. Overcorrections show areas in which Karen reread the text to correct a miscue that did not need correcting because it made sense in the story. This drop in percentile is a strength for Karen. It shows that rather than attending to each and every word, she is reading the text and monitoring for meaning

Her high scores on graphic similarity and sound similarity still suggest an overreliance on the graphophonic cuing system. Karen is very concerned with accuracy in her oral reading. On these measures, her overreliance on graphical features did not appear to interfere with her construction of meaning.

Throughout the year, there were many opportunities to observe Karen's speaking competencies and her oral literacies. The children took turns sharing and reading a daily poem. They shared in author's chair, presented con-

	October	April
Meaning Construction	73%	80%
No loss	58%	76%
Partial loss	15%	4%
Loss	27%	20%
Grammatical Relations	80%	84%
Strength	50%	76%
Partial strength	20%	4%
Overcorrection	10%	4%
Weakness	20%	16%
Graphic Relations	96%	100%
Sound Relations	89%	96%

Table 5-5. Comparison of Reading Miscue Statistics

tent area reports, spoke in literature discussion groups, participated in class meetings, read their family stories at our class family nights, and organized and presented a workshop on writing family stories at another elementary school out of our district.

On the occasions when Karen read from her text, I observed that she read fluently and with expression. Often she utilized props with her presentations, such as pictures or artifacts. On one occasion, she presented her science topic in a game show format and brought in game show prizes for the class to receive if they answered her correctly.

The poems that she chose to read were frequently from the works of Shel Silverstein and she read them with humor and laughter. I noted in my journal frequently that Karen does not go into a reading "cold." She sits with the text and practices her reading continuously until she is comfortable with her oration. In many cases, such as presentations, she practiced so long that she completed her presentation from memory—but kept her note cards in her pocket just in case.

Karen entered our classroom as a shy reluctant reader. She lacked confidence in herself and in her reading ability. She did not believe that she read well, nor did she believe that she possessed the ability to be what she would consider a "good" reader. Through her reading and classroom experiences with literature, Karen emerged as a strong, confident reader in both reality and self-perception.

References

Avi. 1990. *The True Confessions of Charlotte Doyle.* NY: Orchard Press.

Day, A. 1988. *Frank & Ernest.* NY: Scholastic.

Morra, M., and Potts, E. 1994. *Choices.* NY: Avon Books.

Schwartz, C. L., Hobbie, W. L., Constine, L. S., and Ruccione, K. S. 1994. *Survivors of Childhood Cancer.* St. Louis, MO: Mosby.

Scieszka, J. 1991. *The Knights of the Kitchen Table.* NY: Viking Press. and 1989. *The True Story of the Three Little Pigs.* NY: Viking Kestrel.

Spinelli, J. 1990. *Maniac Magee.* NY: Little, Brown & Co., Inc.

Tomlinson, C. M., and Lynch-Brown, C. 1996. *Essentials of Children's Literature.* Needham Heights, MA: Allyn & Bacon.

White, E. B. 1952. *Charlotte's Web.* NY: Dell.

Notes

1. This time period covers approximately 405 days of school. Karen was in school 173 days and absent 232 days. This does not account for the days that she arrived at school and was sent home early.

2. Schwartz, et. al., 1994; Morra and Potts, 1994.

3. All words followed by an asterisk mean that Karen circled this word inferring that she thinks it is not spelled conventionally.

4. These words are represented by a * symbol.

5. In Karen's original journal the word *outrageous* falls at the end of a line and cannot be completed. She hyphenates the word conventionally (out-) and moves onto the next line.

6. Jon Scieszka's book *The True Story of the Three Little Pigs.*

7. 1990 Newbery Winner. It is marketed for children ages 9–12 according to Tomlinson and Lynch-Brown, 1996.

8. Day, 1988.

9. White, 1952.

10. Scieszka, 1991.

11. Avi, 1990.

6

A Classroom Literacy Program for All Students

In two weeks, my summer break ends and I begin teaching my own K1[1] class. Since this is not my first year teaching a multiage class or a kindergarten and first grade combination, I will have the advantage of knowing where to start. I have schedules to look at, curtains to make, and a great deal of curriculum to write.

When writing my curriculum I need to make sure that it accommodates all of my children and is flexible enough to individualize to their specific needs. My planning will need to be separated into three different focus areas. I must create a learning program that:

- accommodates individual needs
- incorporates all of the mandated standards and requirements
- supports and sustains ongoing assessment, individualization, and growth.

Let's start with the first challenge.

Accommodating Individual Needs

Think about the children in your classroom. Who needs modified materials? More direct instruction? More instruction in general? How will we accommodate these needs? These are all questions we work out over time as we come to know our children.

At the beginning of the year, we are not afforded this advanced knowledge. We look at our class lists and try to ascertain what negotiations will need to be made ahead of time to accommodate certain needs. We don't know Karen, or Kiev, or Tony yet. It seems impossible to plan, but it's not. We can respond proactively and prepare for various situations. All we need are materials and flexibility.

As a rule of thumb, I require materials that accommodate a developmental range of approximately two years below through two years above the grade level that I am teaching. For example, if I am teaching the third grade, I will need enough materials to accommodate reading levels from first grade through fifth grade—at a minimum. When planning and/or writing my curriculum, I must coordinate my materials to my various developmental levels and needs. All of my children must participate in the same content study. Therefore, if we are studying the Civil War time period, Tony can read a beginning novel or chapter book on Abe Lincoln. I know there is one in the second grade reading series. Romaro (in the gifted program) can design a research project on Civil War forts. He can work on his library research skills at the same time. Karen could read about the Underground Railroad. She is interested in how the songs and quilts carried clues to the runaway slaves. There is a story of Harriet Tubman in one of our history books that is within her independent reading level. All of the children can use the computer and help each other. As a teacher, you must think in advance. Materials are one of the keys to unity and individualization.

The other is flexibility. We need to make sure that the curricular program we create will have built-in individualization and flexibility in its work samples, expectations, teaching styles, and time frames. We will need to create flexible schedules and structures to accommodate any pull-out instruction still deemed necessary and the various rates and ways that people work. We will need to assign and generate projects that allow for personalization of the finished product. Tony can dress like Abe Lincoln and discuss his life as Abe. Karen can create a new quilt pattern with a hidden message. Romaro can present a computer slide show of forts.

It is our ultimate goal to create a curricular program that allows us to teach all of our children at their various levels seamlessly and effortlessly with one curriculum. In addition, this curriculum must meet all of the necessary guidelines and requirements. Let's address the issue of accountability next.

Accountability

When creating an instructional program we must make sure that we have built-in accountability for documentation and evaluation. Our first imperative is our responsibility to create programs which implement all federal, state, and district curriculum standards. We will begin writing our curriculum here.

Objective 1

To incorporate state, district and curriculum benchmarks, and standards, you will need:

- all district curriculum guidelines for your grade level
- all state standards that pertain to your grade level
- a list of all of the required assessments for your grade level and the content they cover
- teacher editions and resource materials for every adopted content area textbook at your grade level
- knowledge of the depth of coverage and content material taught in the grades before and after the grades you teach
- knowledge of developmental approximations and expectations based upon your class population and grade level
- general knowledge of the social and cultural interests of the children you teach
- a list of items and areas you would like to teach
- all of your class schedules for lunch, special activities, pull-out instruction, band, and so on
- pencils
- an eraser
- lots of paper

Ready?

Step 1 While reviewing your state and district curriculum requirements, write down all of the required content material to be covered this year.

List each content area separately. Go through and write down all of the subskills and benchmarks required for each area.[2] Now, looking at these subskills, are there any that can be grouped together or flow together naturally? A good way to find common threads among curriculum is to plot the required concept areas out onto Venn diagrams. Where are your overlaps and connections? These are good places to start looking when you are searching for commonalities to plan an integrated theme or unit.

Now, take another sheet of paper. Write down the broad categories we just identified that encompass most of the required content.

For example, three of my required content areas are to teach letter writing, simple tools, and American History (from the Colonial to Civil War period). I can fit all of these concepts together under the broad heading of *History of Colonization.* Under this umbrella we could look at the simple tools the new colonists required and how they were made. We could write letters back to England as Pilgrims and diary entries as slaves.

I would now take my broad category, History of Colonization, and look to see what other content requirements might lend themselves towards this theme. I am sure there are many science and math concepts that could figure naturally into a colonization scenario (nutrition, health, foliage, map reading, celestial navigation, measuring, etc.). The grouped areas I create must complement each other or relate to each other naturally. They cannot be forced.

In the primary grades, kindergarten through second grade, I create my curriculum themes by beginning with the required science content. Almost everything we do in the younger grades is social studies. By coming to school and learning to navigate their worlds, the children incorporate and apply most of the required social studies skills and criteria. The science concepts for the children do not apply themselves so incidentally. We may talk about the weather every day. We look at the weather before we go outside, home, to recess, or PE. But there is a difference between talking about the weather and studying the weather. The latter requires a more focused, structured discussion. If my children need to identify three different types of clouds, then a general knowledge of the weather is not good enough for these purposes. By using the science requirements as my framework, I can then see how the social studies criteria lends itself naturally to the required science subareas.

My literature sets and language arts themes and criteria will now attempt to revolve around and complement the identified science theme areas. The math criteria, like the social studies criteria, will be integrated naturally. Its concepts could complement our science theme areas or simply help us navigate our everyday world.

In the older grades, third grade through sixth grade, I begin writing my curriculum with the required subskills from the social studies content rather than the science. I find that in the older grades the social studies content requires a more direct focus of attention. The criteria for social studies in the older grades are not incidental, functional knowledge. By utilizing literature in these instances, the material comes to life. It allows the children to focus on the individual stories that relate to the historical, political, and cultural makings of our world. The math concepts can then be integrated easily as they fit naturally into the various themes or related content areas.

The science criteria are treated separately if they cannot be integrated into the social studies content. For instance, when you are studying the colonial period and need to cover the rain forest, then it will need to be taught and treated separately. In these situations, I usually handle the uncovered required material as inquiries and employ a research/project type format. The morning is our language/history block, and the afternoon is the content math and inquiry block.

Once I have listed all of my required concepts for either science or social studies and have brainstormed some possible thematic connections, I am ready to incorporate some of the remaining factors of consideration.

Step 2 Look at all required assessments and write down the test objectives, formats, and content covered.

In the primary grades, I am mostly dealing with district required reading material assessments and the state and national norm-referenced tests of achievement, which test general grade level knowledge in all subject areas.

The required reading tests are usually derived from the district's adopted reading textbook series, commonly referred to as a basal series. Each district and school has their individual criteria for which tests need to be completed and/or introduced, but usually the classroom teacher is required to obtain a reading testing sample from the beginning, middle, and end of the school year. This usually translates into making sure that at a minimum your children have completed the required theme tests and readings for the first theme of the year, the last theme of the year, and the thematic unit that falls around mid-year (January). These tests are usually required documentation kept in the child's academic folder.

Look at the topics of the required readings and see how these can be related to your area of study at the required times of year. If the topics do not mesh with your content study, then you can treat the reading test as direct instructional time in test-taking skills, story elements, and reading test formats. During your shared reading times and writing workshop mini-lessons, you can focus on one of the tested areas and see how it can be employed in your morning picture book or daily poem. Ask the children, "What is the main idea of the section I just read in teacher read aloud?" "How do you know?" "How would you answer that on a test?" Show the children what this learning looks like with other materials so that they may make associations and fine-tune their generalizations.

Most reading tests ask the child to respond to a prior knowledge activity by looking at the title and drawing and writing their predictions to the story. Comprehension is frequently assessed by the child's ability to follow character or plot development over time and is predominately measured by a drawing accompanied by short answer responses. The inferential questions the children are responding to can be determined by the stories' text and illustrations. Phonemic awareness, spelling, and skills of convention are generally handled through multiple-choice formats. There is usually some type of authentic looking print like a letter or a newspaper article that the children need to edit for convention. The tests generally end with a personal response and opinion to the story.

I need to prepare my children for these various test formats and the ways in which they will be required to respond. In addition to the content criteria, they need to be comfortable with these testing measures and formats. Preparing my children for the format of the testing becomes an area we focus on when we discuss reading and writing strategies for various purposes. For the reading series tests, I need to make sure that my children are competent with various strategies and skills, such as decoding, editing, and locating information in text.

I now know what specific content and testing knowledge I need to incorporate throughout the school year. This is my accountability and the ways in which my children are assessed. I must make sure that they feel competent, are competent, and can look smart on the official tests. They must be able to independently transfer and apply their everyday knowledge to these various testing situations and formats.

Step 3 Go through all of the adopted textbooks and available teaching resources.

You should do this for two purposes. The first is to identify all of the objectives that the adopted textbook is said to teach and that the children are required to learn. Write these down and keep them with your district and state accountability checklists. Peruse these as you search to see what your program encompasses naturally and what could be used for inquiry, whole class, mini-lessons, or individual instruction. The reading textbook's skills can serve as a weekly planning reminder as to what items may lend themselves naturally to mini-lessons or shared reading conversations.

The second reason to go through the textbooks is to establish available teaching materials. Since I want to make sure that I have the resources to teach my created curriculum, I'll need to look through all textbook manuals and resource aids. I'll also look through my literature sets, leveled book sets, poetry, songs, games, magazines, picture books, professional books, science and math supplies, community resources, and media supplies. I want to make sure that it will not cost me a fortune or impose outrageous time expectations searching and creating materials.

While I am investigating all of these materials, I will regroup them into a rubberized tub, label them by theme, and store them until I employ each unit. This way I can add to the units as I gather material from year to year. And, when it comes time to implement a thematic unit, I can use the storage tub as part of my planning structure. The various materials inside will remind me to incorporate the diverse domains and learning styles as well as the varied intelligences and individual needs.

Now that I know what I want to teach, I need to turn my focus towards the children.

Step 4 Acquire knowledge of depth of content coverage and materials in the grades before and after the grade you teach.

I need to start my children where they are comfortable in their learning and connect the new to the known. To do this, I need to know where they are going and where they have been. I also need to know other information, which is discussed in the following sections.

Step 5 Acquire knowledge of developmental approximations.

I need to be familiar with developmental stages of literacy and learning so that I can form some expectations regarding the developmental levels and interests of the students I teach. Using stages of approximate development, I can determine a fairly good starting point for lessons and instructional materials. I need to make sure that I begin where everybody can be successful. These whole class generalizations will be continuously fine-tuned to individual children as time goes by. As I learn the needs of each child, I will be able to attend to their specific demonstrated performances and areas of strengths, weaknesses, and interests. This knowledge will allow me to plan each child's academic learning experiences as will the information in Step 6.

Step 6 Acquire knowledge of social and cultural issues of the children you teach.

What TV shows do your students like? Who are their heroes? What are their interests? What is their home life like? What worries do they have when they leave the classroom? Who supports them at home? How can they relate to your curriculum? Who will have materials to complete their schoolwork, money for fieldtrips, or money for lunch? What are the family expectations and goals for your children?

Every single thing in our children's lives will affect their education and their learning. The more we know about our students, the more we can adapt our teaching to accommodate their needs. A curriculum that employs many structures, yet remains flexible and open-ended, allows us to establish whole class procedures, routines, and expectations while individualizing instruction.

Individualizing instruction also includes accommodating the personal interests and enjoyments of the teacher and the children. Curriculum needs to be engaging and interesting if it is to be nurtured and grow.

Step 7 Now that you have a list of all of the requirements, create a "want" list of the topics that you would have fun teaching. Include the areas that you think your children would also like to learn. For example, your list could include lizards, Abraham Lincoln, and so on.

Using this list, go back to Step 1. Look at the thematic units we brainstormed for our required content materials. Are any of the things we want to teach or learn incorporated or reflected in these brainstormed units? If not, start over. This time work with Steps 7 and 1 simultaneously. In order to plan the theme criteria, your concepts must be from your want list. Try to work your required content into your desired unit topic.

Once we know what it is we are going to teach, we can turn our thoughts to *how* we are going to teach it. This brings us to our next focus area. We are going to totally switch gears here. So far we have looked at ways to create our curriculum based upon required content and the ways that children learn. It's time to look at how the curriculum we just created is going to allow us to accommodate all regular and mainstreamed children as well as individualized instruction, and identify and assess our children's needs. What does learning look like in this setting?

Accommodating Children

Objective 2

A successful curriculum supports and sustains ongoing assessment, individualization, and growth.

I need to make sure that our curricular program accommodates all of the individual needs, all of the various levels of development, all of the diverse interests and learning styles, and a flexible schedule. At the same time, it requires a daily routine with known expectations and procedures to provide a structure for both the children and me.

The curriculum must include a daily shared reading, reading and writing workshop, teacher read aloud, independent reading opportunities, and an inquiry-based content study. It must allow for whole class, small group, and one-to-one instruction with flexible groupings. It must encourage and support: community, autonomy, effort, ownership, ongoing assessment, practice, and personal responsibility. In Chapter 4, we looked at an overall structure of my class day from the perspective of providing a balanced literacy program. In this section, we are going to look at some of the actual instruction I implement in the classroom that allows me the structure, flexibility, and accountability in my program.

The first element I must attend to is the physical environment of my classroom. It must support my philosophy and methods of teaching. The room must accommodate areas for whole class instruction, small group work, independent work, cooperative groupings, and autonomous centers or stations. It must be an inviting, homey atmosphere that relaxes the soul and nurtures growth, democracy, acceptance, respect, value, risk taking, literacy, and self-worth.

The Classroom Environment and Setting

I will need areas for writing supplies, independent reading books, math manipulatives, listening center materials, science inquiry materials, puppets, art supplies, a free-time area, language arts manipulatives, an area for shared reading and whole class instruction, and seating for twenty-five children split into groups of four. These areas must be created so that they provide structure for both me and the children. The classroom must allow for autonomy and individuality. The children must be able to work creatively at their own pace without constant support from me. I must find time to focus on individual and small group instruction without constant interruption. I also do not want to give the children any worksheet type materials where everybody is doing the same task. Worksheets are not individualized and they only examine a lower level of knowing (based upon Bloom's Taxonomy[3]). There are more literate ways of keeping the children occupied and engaged so that I can teach.

Everything in my room must provide a learning opportunity. The children are grouped in sets of four to facilitate cooperative learning, social skills, and the art of conversation and discussion. They problem-solve academically and socially among themselves and learn how to discuss and respect the opinions of their peers. And, I know that by talking amongst themselves, they are increasing their listening comprehension and subsequent reading potential.

There is a whole class area for shared reading, math lessons, comfortable independent reading, class gatherings, and so on. This area must also allow for a whiteboard or blackboard, a reading chair, and a carpet. Because most reading groups are conducted here, there should be some space for miscellaneous teacher supplies, checklists, the teacher read aloud novel, and copies of the books being read in literature groups.

Classroom materials are a key factor in accommodating needs. Varied materials are extremely important for establishing risk taking, comfort, and acceptance. It must be as acceptable for a sixth grader to read a Big Book in a read aloud activity as it is for him or her to read an encyclopedia. The more choices of materials, the more varied the need, interest, experimentation, and developmental level I can accommodate. Some basic materials you may wish to include are:

- **The writing area** needs to contain writing supplies, publishing materials, writing ideas, and address books. There needs to be an area to store all of the writing workshop notebooks throughout the year and folders or portfolios for finished pieces of oversized, bulky work that is still in progress.

- **The art area** needs to contain a plethora of varied craft and supply items.

- **The science area** needs to provide space for us to complete our weekly science observations and establish a discovery zone where found treasures, such as plants, seeds, nests, mold, bugs, magnets, and eggshells, are kept and explored. Science-related books are great to keep here as well as some magnifying glasses, a scale, some lab coats, measuring tape, and some clipboards.

- **The math area** needs to accommodate various math-related materials. The children should be able to access the materials they wish to work with as needed. This means that I must have an area that contains such items as games, manipulatives, calculators, and so on.

How to Handle the Content Areas

Math Most of my directed teaching of math is conducted with the whole group on the carpet. I use the adopted math textbook for the worksheet type math practices and assessments that we may employ. Typically, after looking at all of the requirements and integrating as best as I can, I determine what will need to be taught more directly. I then jump from textbook to textbook as needed. However, most of the time math is incorporated into an ongoing project like walking the Appalachian trail or planning a garden.

The younger children will spend a great deal of time exploring using manipulatives (both directed and independently) and creating their own understandings of numeracy, place value, estimation, measuring, volume, and patterns. Daily math procedures of voting for lunch, counting out pencils and snack materials, creating word problems out of our morning attendance, graphing preferences, creating Venn diagrams, searching for patterns, and participating in daily calendar activities are structures that allow for ongoing interaction, involvement, individualization, observation, and assessment of growth over time. These open-ended activities lead to familiarity, repetition, and routine for the children. These structures encourage experimentation, autonomy, and problem solving at the child's developmental level. The children can participate at any level.

We can individualize instruction further by seeking out simple ways to help our children become independent. For example, by using graph paper instead of notebook paper for addition and subtraction problems, we can help the children line up their numerals to retain the integrity of place value. This helps younger children grasp the concept that maintaining place value is important. It also helps children with spatial problems keep numbers in proper columns.

Karen maintained a file box that worked as her memory. One section was devoted to math operations. It contained step-by-step procedures (with examples) of how to do such things as long division, adding and subtracting mixed fractions, and so on. Use of her file box for assessments was written into her IEP as an accommodating strategy. Karen could do the math required. She just couldn't remember that she knew how. The mere presence of the file box gave her control, comfort, ownership, and autonomy.

What can you show your children that will help them continue their learning when you are not around to help? What arsenal of supplies can you give them?

Language Arts

It helps to remember that when it comes to our daily lives and the language arts, almost everything we do incorporates or utilizes listening, speaking, reading, or writing. It would be nearly impossible to accomplish anything without applying one of these four domains. We are always using the language arts.

With each new or different exposure to these domains our schema is broadened and we are better able to assimilate and accommodate new learnings in various situations. We problem solve using appropriate literacy strategies and interactions depending upon our need and setting. We participate and observe in a working literate environment where our exposure to literacy events, and our practices and interactions with print will provide ongoing support and a continuance of learning. When all is said and done: The only way to become a better reader is to read; the only way to become a better writer is to write; and of course, the same is true for speaking and listening. We must be immersed in and practice all four of these literacies with a great deal of simultaneity.

Creating situations that allow for continuous immersion and practice in reading, writing, listening, and speaking for varied purposes should be the core of your literacy program. Children need to be reading, and they need to be writing. The ways to allow for this ownership, progression, practice, choice, and immersion in your literacy program while still allowing you to be accountable, are to apply some direct instruction and substantiate a grade.

Shared Reading As stated in Chapter 4, after the morning announcements, we begin our day with shared reading. To me, this is one of the most important instructional times of our school day. If we get nothing else accomplished today, we *will* do shared reading. This carpet time is more than just a touchy-feely, community-building, aesthetic enhancement of literature. It is the foundation of my entire language arts program.

Through the modeling of the morning picture book, I am able to assess my children's interest, comfort, and participation with print read orally. I am able to observe their listening comprehension and ability to discuss and respond to a story. I can see how my children internalize the print, and the types of interactions they choose to have with the text. While Molly discusses inferences that remind her of when she was little, Tony is just beginning to notice that there are letters in the book that are also in his name. I notice that Karen is using the illustrations as a strategy for making sense of print. She in turn notices the strategies, responses, and interactions of the story generated from her peers. Everybody brings something different to the task.

Through shared reading, we can model various reading strategies, reading behaviors, and teach all of the skills and story elements found in most structured reading programs using our morning picture book (if I choose to). We can model writing strategies that the author used to create such a great story. We can use the book as a springboard to a learning activity in science, or as a springboard to a writing activity, or a model for an individual or class book. We are modeling with real materials that are interesting, transferable to new learning situations, and readily available to use and revisit.

The use of picture books and Big Books in the shared reading experience should be a crucial element in your program for establishing a risk free, cultured learning environment. First of all, they are fun. They are aesthetically beautiful, and everybody loves a good story. Second, many of our regular and special needs students will require narrative and expository materials that they can handle independently, and that we can use in small group or one-to-one situations instructionally. If these are not accepted as a working part of our curriculum, then these materials become an embarrassment and stigma when applied in this manner.

Everyday, following the picture book, we do our morning poem. The poem allows me to see how my children handle print of another genre and how they discuss and illustrate poetry. Because it's on a chart paper format and allows for repetition, we can observe who focuses upon the structures and conventions of the print. Who follows along with text? Who looks at the words? Who has one-to-one correspondence. When we play *What Do We Notice*[4] with the poem, we can observe and assess the strategies the children use and the skills and concrete knowledge they employ and apply. We can model and introduce word families, *daily oral language* activities, colorful language, spelling, the difference between a line and a sentence, dialect, decoding strategies for unknown words, and phonemic awareness.

Depending on each child's developmental level, interest, and place in their learning, everybody will have something different to bring to our literacy events; and everybody will be able to take away something different. I will be able to introduce quality literature and poetry, nonchalantly teach language arts skills and strategies, and observe and assess the children's literacies and behaviors in these areas every morning.

Literature Discussion Groups Literature discussion groups provide for a different type of reading instruction, assessment, and observation. Here we are modeling, observing, and assessing how the students handle printed material when reading independently. We are providing structured opportunities where the children can choose a literature book and after reading it, respond to it. If the ultimate goal of reading is to be able to read and construct meaning by making sense of print, then we need to give the kids opportunities to read and make sense of print. We need to raise their metacognition by bringing the smart things that they are already doing to the surface. We can model what independent readers do before, during, and after reading. We can examine various ways to respond to a text by making it our own. We can appreciate and enjoy literature. (Remember, if a child chooses not to read, he or she may as well be a nonreader.)

Through literature discussion we can individualize instruction by offering more choice and a range of materials. For example, in the primary grades, if we were studying the moon, then Tony may be reading a very simple book, such as *A Child's Goodnight Book*.[5] Debbie could be reading *Papa, Please Get Me the Moon*,[6] and Molly could be reading *The Moon*.[7] In instructional settings, these books could be used in addition to our printed material and leveled books that deal with the moon as the subject.

In the intermediate grades, if we were studying character development and reading books with memorable female characters, Kiev may be reading *The Secret Life of Deborah Samson*,[8] Karen may be reading *Charlotte's Web*,[9] and Teresa may be reading *The True Confessions of Charlotte Doyle*.[10]

We can assess our children's comprehension by watching them read, listening to their interpretations of the story, and looking at their visual responses to the text. All of our children can sit together and discuss the same books or like themes, regardless of ability and current knowledge.

It is my job to support any child who wishes to read any book. If Karen chooses a book that I know will be difficult for her, I may question her choice. The ability to choose books wisely is a literacy task that we need to become competent with. If Karen is aware that the text may be difficult, but wishes to read it anyway, I probably will not override her decision. I know that I offered books at her independent reading and interest level that she did not want to read. I know that this is the book she is interested in because she says that she wants to work through the book anyhow, and I know that she wants to join her classmates who chose the same text.

I also know that motivation, ownership, and acceptance are a powerful force. I am very pleased that literacy is important to Karen, and that she wants to see herself as a reader and be in the same group with her new best friend. She is willing to apply the effort and perseverance, which means she will be open to advances and suggestions of help. I also know that this is just one aspect of our literacy program, and Karen is immersed in real-life print and skill instruction continuously and as needed in other arenas of our program. If Karen works through the book and sits in group, she will be able to see how the children understand the story, and through their discussions, she will have additional support for her reading as well as modeling literature group procedures and ways to respond to print. She will be writing her literature responses into her reading journal, which means I know she will be focusing very heavily on the graphophonics of the text as she copies some of the words, sentences, and title into her journal. During independent reading times, Karen will be able to sit with her literature book and buddy and read with some of her friends in the same group. I can also use her literature book for some of our individual one-on-one focus work.

Literature Group Grades The literature discussion groups allow us to observe the children's interactions with real print. In the intermediate grades, we are able to substantiate and document a minimum of four numerical or letter grades every three weeks for every book read and discussed. For example, Karen will receive one grade for:

1. reading her book according to her contract, following all procedures, journalizing her responses after reading, sharing her responses in the group, participating in the group, and listening and sharing appropriately with her peers.
2. her journal responses at the end of the book when the journals are collected.
3. her reading project she created and shared at the end of the book.
4. the grade on her open-ended book test.

With the primary children, the literature discussion groups revolve around picture books rather than novels. The books are generally carried over a one week period and the children respond differently to the same text each day. Their literature groups meet daily (depending on our schedule) and allow for ongoing current assessment and on-your-feet planning.

Skills Through Literature When using literature for specific instruction, we should not mix real reading pleasure with skill work. We should always appreciate the story and discuss the book. Then, we should revisit the book later for a different purpose—focused instruction based upon a demonstrated individual or group need.

It is very important to establish in your children's minds that skill work is not reading, and reading is not skill work. Always separate the two with the children. We read the story for pleasure first and foremost. This maintains the integrity of *what reading is*; and by having the story read ahead of time, everybody has created a schema and is familiar with the text. If we choose to use the book in a strategic way, we simply revisit it. We revisit the text for a different purpose: to demystify the book and figure out strategies for troublesome areas; and to look at the text as a writer deconstructing the print to see what the author did to make the book so good and create meaning for the reader.

The literature groups are why we read—to appreciate books. The skill sessions are to help us read. A very simple demarcation is all that is necessary. It may be presented like this:

- Wasn't that a great story? I liked it too. Let's look at it again for a minute. I just want to show you something I noticed while I was reading. Do you see over here on this page where he swallows the ocean? The author used the word *gulped*. (Write *gulped* on the whiteboard.) What does this word mean? How do we know? What would or could we do if we came to this word in our reading and we didn't know what it said? How do we solve unknown words? Did the illustrator give us any clues? Look at the letters in the word. It begins with a "*g*." What sound could this letter make? Look at the ending "*ed*." Can we break the word down into parts that we know? And so on.

- Karen do you remember yesterday when we were talking about Kit in *The Witch of Blackbird Pond*,[11] and we had a question about the ....? Can you bring your book and come and sit with me for a minute, I want to show you something. Is this a good time for you to leave your writing or would it be better if I go and sit with Kiev for a little bit and come back to you?

Individualized, Targeted Reading   Guided reading, instructional reading, small group instruction, reading recovery procedures, individual one-on-one focus work—I do not know what to call the more direct instructional times in our reading program. To say that this is my instructional reading time seems to negate the fact that everything we do is for the purposes of instruction and increasing our strategies and schema. So, as far as I am concerned, anytime that I am working with a student for the purpose of progressing their learning; *and* my instruction is based on my knowledge of literacy processes and their ZPD,[12] then I am teaching reading.

When I am working with children individually or in a small group, it is because I have identified a specific area of need that we are going to focus on and practice. This is the time when I have more control over the materials and the activities. I choose the books we use based upon the student's independent reading approximations. The purpose of these instructional times is to work on needs specifically demonstrated by the student. My instruction appears more direct at these times. In these learning situations we will be reading books, writing stories, working on skills and strategies in the context of the book or written story, and employing such things as: cut up sentences, word walls, word sorts, magnetic letters, language experience activities, graphic organizers, book writing, and specific test-taking skills. During this time, I will also administer assessments of running records and miscue analysis as needed. On the days we don't have literature groups, I know I will work with some of the children individually. In addition, by knowing where my children are in their learning, everything, including reading a sign on the way to lunch, becomes a guided reading moment.

Test-Taking Strategies In the intermediate grades, we occasionally spend some time (about ten minutes or so before shared reading) at our seats working on test-taking skills. Typically, I take all of the assessments and workbook skill pages from the adopted reading series and put them on transparencies. I use the reading series as a primary source because they are exact representations of the assessments the children will need to accomplish independently. They also utilize the same bubbling format as our standardized tests. The children read the transparency and secure their answers in their heads. When everybody has had an appropriate amount of time to read and get their answers, we discuss the transparency with the whole class. We deconstruct the assessment. First, we respond to the questions and establish the correct answer. Second, we figure out how the answer was solved, and clear up any misconceptions that arise along the way. Finally, when we are done dissecting the assessment and deciphering the test-maker's tricks, the kids like to share things they noticed on the test—similar to the way they examine the print of a poem.

Independent, Free Choice Reading There are many opportunities for independent, free choice reading. The classroom library supports and respects all kinds of print as legitimate reading materials. Remember, the goal is to get children reading independently so they can and will practice on their own; thus increasing their own literacy without the need for constant adult support. Stopping a child from reading the material they choose or are engaged in simply because I do not deem it educational enough is not only disrespectful, but does not make sense. Reading a comic book or baseball cards can accomplish my goals just as well, if not better, than the novel I would have chosen for the child. This time period is called *independent reading* and the choice of materials should be the child's. If I do not want, trust, or allow my children their choice of school appropriate materials, then I need to call this reading time something else. Observing children and their choices of reading materials is in itself an ongoing assessment of their individual reading behaviors, levels, attitudes, and confidence.

Independent reading is built into other structures of our classroom program. In the younger grades, my children also maintain what we refer to as envelope books.[13] At the beginning of the year, each child receives a giant manila envelope to decorate. Inside the envelope is a one page reading log that accommodates approximately twenty books. The log states the date and the title of the book read. The child's parent then notes whether the book was a *Goldilocks Book*[14] or not. I want to keep the children progressing with books that are *just right*. When the children choose a book to read, they put it in their envelope and bring it home. Depending on the child and the book chosen, I or another classmate may read that book with the child before it goes in the envelope. If it is a book that requires some concentration, such as a new text, then it is important that I read it first with the child so they have a structure that can help them practice, especially if I know there is little support at home. The children will read and practice their envelope books. After practicing, they will read the book to either me or the class. They will then choose a sticker to put on their envelope, and choose another book. I like my children to switch their envelope books at least once a week.

Using envelope books, I can observe my children's book choices, monitor their reading of independent choices, notice their ability to handle various texts, give the children opportunities to choose and practice instructional reading in an independent, risk free setting, and make sure they have something to read in the house that they enjoy.

Mr. Bear is a stuffed bear that goes home with the helper of the day. I use a Paddington Bear[15] because he is a literary character and he comes with a tag asking the *bearer* to please take care of this bear. When we were studying oceans, the class also wanted a Mr. Whale. The helper of the day then got to choose whether they wanted Mr. Bear or Mr. Whale as their evening companion.

Mr. Bear goes home with the helper of the day inside his own Mr. Bear backpack. Inside the backpack with Mr. Bear is a folder that contains the child's share sheet for the next day of school. The child brings Mr. Bear home and at sometime that evening introduces him to their family and reads him a story. After reading, the child records the date and title of the book on his or her share sheet. They (Mr. Bear and the child) then write and/or draw about their favorite part of the story. The child discusses his or her share sheet with the class the following day. The share sheets are kept in our Mr. Bear three-ring notebook to read and look at during independent reading times.

Daily Calendar Time For the primary children, there is a great deal of language arts learning and teaching that can take place during our math calendar time. Our math calendar time takes place in a whole group setting near the math calendar bulletin board area. Pulling from calendar activities employed from *Mathematics Their Way*[16] and various mathematics textbooks, we are exposed to the same daily print and procedures through the context of math. This repetition of print and repeated modeling of strategies provides a scaffold for the emergent reader, and opportunities to explore for the independent reader.

While doing calendar activities, we can individualize instruction depending upon the task and the child. For example, if Tony were making today's date out of coins (the 12th), he may choose to make it with twelve pennies. Shelby may see that she can make twelve with a dime and two pennies; and Sarah may notice that she can trade Shelby's dime for two nickels. Rashan may notice that the number twelve has a two in it; and Jenny may notice that the word penny starts with a "p." These are all factors that identify their zone of proximal development (ZPD). Each day I should be able to observe some growth or progress on somebody's part. If not, I need to rethink my program.

The math calendar as well as many daily classroom routines also provide constant practice and interaction with print. By participating in the morning calendar activity, we are practicing daily with:

- repeated, predictable text
- identifying, reading, and deriving meaning from words and print in our environment for functional purposes
- applying reading strategies and skills in context
- increasing vocabulary, use, and sight word comprehension of math related language
- connecting and noticing patterns of language
- interpreting words into number sentences and number sentences into words
- creating real-life word problems
- discussing and making sense of our world through different forms of print

Writing Workshop In writing workshop, I have an opportunity to observe my children's writing behaviors and performance from brainstorming to finished product, July through June.[17] I can see their growth, their practices and revisions, their choices, their problem solving, their spellings, their conventions, their approximate level of development, and where I should go in my instruction. This writing portfolio is used as data and record keeping materials for report cards and conferences as well as writing IEPs.

By allowing the children to generate and create print, we are supporting the authors in their writing context. Their individual creations, the open-ended nature, and the autonomy of the writing workshop allows for individual growth and flexible schedules. It allows me to negotiate work and adjust expectations without complaints of fairness or comparison among the children.

To support ongoing literacy practices:

- we maintain two or three author bags in the classroom for checkout. These bags may go home with students who wish to create stories or illustrations in the evenings. The bags contain supplies typically desired by any author and illustrator.

- journals are used at different times for various intents. Sometimes we will employ morning journals, which are used for free responses and sharing with peers. I've used math journals, science journals, dialogue journals, reading response journals, and diaries. These are all authentic ways to use various forms of print for different functions and combinations.

- class sharings, memo boards, class books, pen pals, research projects, class newspapers, mailboxes, invitations, posters, greeting cards, and thank you notes are all authentic ways to incorporate writing into our daily routine.

- we focus on writing and producing text in a more expository genre with the younger children. The children maintain a Science Observation Log. We examine a chosen object and identify its basic attributes of size, shape, color, texture, and weight. Each week we record our observations on a log sheet and keep them in our folder. During our weekly science observations, the children work through the scientific processes and employ literacy strategies for different authentic purposes.

In the domain of the language arts, the science observation allows us to:

- read repeated, predictable text
- identify, read, and derive meaning from words and print in our environment for functional purposes
- apply reading strategies and skills in context
- increase vocabulary, use, and sight word comprehension of science related language
- connect and notice patterns of language
- interpret senses of sight, sound, smell, touch, and taste into words
- discuss and make sense of our world through different forms of print

This science log also provides data for informing me of the child's ZPD and development over time.

Content Area Inquiry Projects Besides acquiring specific knowledge, inquiry-based content study allows many opportunities for immersion, exploration, and practice in expository writing and reading. The children will be reading and creating print for a different purpose or intent. They will need to locate information and synthesize it into a presentation form. Karen may choose to outline her presentation and present it in the form of a speech. Kiev may use overhead transparencies and draw most of his representations. Molly may choose to act out her inquiry through music, art, and drama.

Although each child goes through similar literacy acts of retrieving and synthesizing information from various resources, their products are individualized and their own. They are physical representations of the child's authentic developmental zone. Where on Bloom's Taxonomy does their project work fall? Is it a very literal project—cut and dry? How creative is their project? How creatively can they manipulate and use print? What is the child's effort and attitude like? Is this their best work?

Remember, our job is one of coach and supporter. We are the ones who must be proactive and ask the questions of our children. We cannot just assign an inquiry project and then wait for the due dates. We must help our children learn how to organize and plan long-term projects and break these goals into smaller manageable objectives.

I need to show Karen various ways to organize her materials and keep notes. Kiev needs to see some ways to take notes. Molly wants to work on taking her notes and making them look like something she wants to share and say. My job is to continually move around and ask, "How can I help you?"

Besides gaining content knowledge, the student learns to:

- produce outlines, graphs, webs
- read for a specific purpose
- locate and use reference materials
- organize notes and create a cohesive text
- employ all stages of the writing process interactively as needed
- bring a writing piece to completion in published form
- create a written and visual project from materials learned
- present their project to the class
- employ listening and public speaking skills
- employ skimming and scanning strategies
- take responsibility for their own learning

All inquiry projects and tests receive two grades. One grade is for the content of the paper. How well did they respond to their inquiry? How accurate and thorough is it? Is this the child's best work? A second grade is received for the conventions of the paper. How well did they bring this piece to final form? The latter grade will be included in their writing scores from writing workshop and other written graded assignments. It is very common to see a student receive a grade of A/D or D/A. It may be that in the first case the child presented a great project, but the mechanics were not corrected. The paper it is written on may be half-ripped out of a notebook with smudges all over it. It may not be in their neatest handwriting, sentences may not be capitalized consistently, and there may be common spelling errors. No other drafts may accompany this paper as required. This is not an acceptable finished piece of writing.

On the other hand, for instance, Kiev might have turned in a beautiful paper. Every single thing is perfect. Except, he didn't answer the question.

Assessment

Kid Watching[18]

Two kindergartners, Jenny, an ESOL student, and Romaro were sitting at their seats working on their morning journals. Romaro was trying to figure out how to spell February. As I walked by, I heard Jenny say to Romaro, "Well, you can turn around and look at the word on the blackboard, you can use your ear spelling, or you can close your eyes and read it in your mind."

Jenny is from Laos. She has been with us in the classroom for only six months. I am always concerned about whether she and my other children are receiving an adequate amount of individual instruction. I relaxed a little after overhearing that conversation.

From their talk, I learned that Jenny is using strategies. Not only is she using strategies, but she is aware of her own literacy processes to verbalize and share them with a classmate. Jenny knows ways to deconstruct and make sense of print, which is our ultimate goal of instruction. I am comfortable in continuing the pace, frequency, and types of instruction I have been using with Jenny. I know I will need to pay attention to some of her specific areas of need, such as letter recognition or phonemic awareness. These are highly tested areas and Jenny will need to perform well on these tested formats in order to show others the knowledge that she has and employs.

Jenny is a risk taker. She continues to show growth in her school work, and she verbalizes strategies for spelling unknown words. For real-life literacy purposes, I think Jenny will be just fine.

And let's not forget Romaro. Romaro has just shown me what he needs from me. I now have a clearer picture of where he is in his development, and where we need to go.

Let's look at Karen.

Karen and Logan are co-leaders of their inquiry group. The class is in the midst of preparing projects for final presentation and I overhear Logan tell Karen not to "worry about it" because he already took care of everything and it is fine. He handed Karen a piece of notebook paper with some writing on it and walked away. As I watch from my position as a literature discussion group member, I see Karen look at the paper for a few minutes, put it down, and cross the room to Logan. In her hand is a stack of index cards. She sits down and after a brief discussion he pulls out a piece of paper and they begin to work together on something.

Logan is a student in the gifted program. He is a very athletic class leader who bursts with confidence and machismo. Karen, of course, is very meek and unassuming. Obviously, there appeared to be a conflict and I was curious to see what was happening. I was also wondering how Karen would handle a situation of confrontation independently. When our literature group broke up, I went over to Karen who was now working independently. I asked her what was up; what was she working on? She simply informed me that Logan tried to take over the group, but the work he did didn't even make sense, so she straightened it out. No big deal.

I'm so very proud of her. She has the confidence of a reader and a writer to approach a *gifted* intimidating male and tell him she has a better idea. Karen too, will be just fine.

Every observable behavior becomes an anecdotal record. These moments document successful literacy behaviors, which can never be put into benchmarks or numbers. They complete the total picture of the child. We can now feel and see the child's voice. They become alive to us. Without our observations, our children will be represented by numbers on a page. They deserve a face. Kid watching is our way of identifying ZPDs and maintaining a total picture of the child.

Establishing Grades

Establishing concrete grades in these areas is not difficult. I have learned to simplify matters throughout the years. I first establish with my children and parents that I thoroughly understand that what I am observing is just the tip of the iceberg. It is not a direct reflection of the child's ability. I have no way of knowing the problem solving and thinking that is going on in the heads of our children unless they tell me. If they are not standing in front of me, I can only assess what it is that I see—not what I think to be true. I know that grades are only a measure of that child's performance on that material at that given place and time. Our program has many opportunities for the children to show their literacies and strengths, and it is my job to see that that occurs. As long as there are grades, I must establish this trust and understanding to maintain the integrity of my program.

I am accountable for stating to the best of my ability what that child's performance looks like at that moment in time. If somebody from the state department of education came in and had to grade a paper or a project, what grade would it be? What does an "A" look like? What does a "C" look like? In grading all nonstandardized materials, I individualize the grade to the child who created the work. I know Karen's work. I know Molly's work. I know Kiev's work. I know everybody's work and what we have been working on up to this point. I know what is excellent, good, and poor effort for every child in my class.

Based on this information I grade my students in this way:

- An "A": If Karen's assignment was absolutely without a doubt great for Karen, and she followed all directions and criteria, she received an "A."
- A "B": If Karen's assignment was really well done for Karen, and she followed all of the directions and criteria, she received a "B."
- A "C": If Karen's assignment was average for Karen, and she followed all of the directions and criteria, she received a "C."
- A "D": If Karen's assignment was below average for Karen, even if she followed most of the directions and criteria, she received a "D."
- An "F": If any child was without an assignment or submitted work that showed little effort, respect, concern, or personal responsibility, they received an "F."

When I was teaching in Arizona, we gave numerical grades instead of letter grades. Let's see how this translates by looking at one of Karen's "A" assignments.

Karen has an "A" on her latest project. It is excellent for Karen. But how excellent is it? There are usually two different grading skills in the elementary school depending on where you live. In some areas an A equals 90 through 100. In other areas an A equals 94 through 100. Karen lived in Arizona where the grading scale of A equals 90 through 100. I am going to take that "A" and break it into even smaller sections:

1. Looking at Karen's paper, does she have a high A? Is it just about a perfect paper? If so, then she would probably score a 97, 98, 99, or 100.

2. Looking at Karen's paper, is it a nice solid A? Are there just a couple of little things that could be fixed or improved? If you are still proud of this work, then she would probably score a 96, 95, 94, or 93.

3. Looking at Karen's paper, how strong is that A? Did she just go over the top producing *good* work and on her way to trying more things? If so, then she would probably score a 92, 91, or 90.

By establishing numerical equivalents for high, middle, and low letter grades, my assessing and accounting for my grades is much easier to complete and explain.

Once we have our first set of grades for all content areas, we can then use these grades as a determination of growth or progress over time, rather than as a statement of their exact literacy ability.

References

Avi. 1990. *The True Confessions of Charlotte Doyle.* NY: Orchard Press.

Baretta-Lorton, M. 1995. *Mathematics Their Way.* NY: Addison-Wesley.

Bloom, B. 1956. *Taxonomy of Educational Objectives, Handbook 1: Cognitive Domain.* NY: McKay.

Bond, M. 1968. *A Bear Called Paddington.* NY: Yearling Books.

Brown, M. W. 1992. *A Child's Good Night Book.* NY: HarperCollins Juvenile Books.

Carle, E. 1986. Papa, *Please Get Me the Moon.* NY: Simon & Schuster.

Fischer, B. 1995. *Thinking and Learning Together: Curriculum and Community in a Primary Classroom.* Portsmouth, NH: Heinemann.

Gibbons, G. 1997. *The Moon Book.* NY: Holiday House.

Goodman, Y. M. 1985. "Kid-Watching: Observing Children in the Classroom." In A. Jaggar and M. Smith-Burke's *Observing the Language Learner.* Newark, DE: International Reading Association.

McGovern, A. 1975. *Secret Soldier: The Story of Deborah Samson.* NY: Scholastic.

Speare, E. G. 1958. *The Witch of Blackbird Pond*. Boston, MA: Houghton Mifflin.

Vygotsky, L. S. 1978. *Mind in Society: The Development of Higher Psychological Processes*. Cambridge, MA: Harvard University Press.

White, E. B. 1958. *Charlotte's Web*. NY: Dell.

Notes

1. A multiage kindergarten and first grade combination.
2. Don't forget other content areas that may be required, such as health, computer science, physical education, and so on.
3. Bloom, 1956.
4. Chapter 4.
5. Brown, 1992 (low ability).
6. Carle, 1986 (medium performance).
7. Gibbons, 1997 (high performance).
8. McGovern, 1975 (low performance).
9. White, 1952 (medium performance).
10. Avi, 1990 (high performance).
11. Speare, 1958.
12. Vygotsky, 1978.
13. Envelope books and Mr. Bear are two ideas that I have accumulated, morphed, and taken from various readings and interactions. I am no longer sure where these came from. My best guess would be that they were introduced from the work of Bobbi Fischer.
14. A Goldilocks Book is a term I accredit to Dr. Karri Williams in Orlando. As one of my reading professors, she consistently referred to the appropriate independent reading level of text through the perspective of Goldilocks. Was the book: too hard, too easy, or just right?
15. Bond, 1968.
16. Baratta-Lorton, 1995.
17. I teach at a year-round school.
18. Goodman, Y. M., 1985.

7

An Exemplary Schoolwide Literacy Program

Goals

1. To have all children reach their literacy potential.
2. To have all children perform independently at their appropriate grade level in the language arts area.
3. To consistently see a "year's growth" as determined by formal and informal assessments.
4. To increase test-taking skills.
5. To create lifelong readers and writers.

In order for teachers to advocate and support their students, the school must support them. A literacy program consisting of the goals I have described may not be allowed, valued, understood, or easy to implement if the school in which we teach is too traditionally based—in either body or soul.

There will be constant tension with regard to scheduling, availability of materials and resources, acceptance of assessments and professional judgment, and explaining and justifying our programs. The school will be testing and evaluating our children in one way, and we'll be teaching them in another.

As a classroom teacher, undergraduate professor, and school reading specialist, I have experienced and observed many situations where lack of consistency throughout the school was the primary reason for reading problems. Individual teaching and instruction in the classrooms looked great, but each teacher valued something different with regard to what literacy was and how it should be evaluated. There was little continuity for the children from grade to grade in instruction, expectations, or classroom measures. A child who was skilled and drilled one year was required to produce holistically the next (and vice versa). Resource teachers were left to figure out how to accommodate the system, teachers, and children. The teachers stood alone, the parents were confused, and the kids just did what they were told. And, as long as the test scores were good and parent complaints were few—from the school's perspective, there really wasn't a problem.

To support the literacies of our children, teachers and administrators need to unite to establish goals, beliefs, and strategies for implementing literacy programs based upon sound classroom practice and the way children learn. It is important to implement schoolwide strategies that will support the teachers in the classroom and best benefit the children. If I were in charge of these critical decisions, I would:

1. Implement a schoolwide staff development program in the language arts.
2. Establish standardized schoolwide measures and assessments that support the school's language arts program.
3. Implement a Title 1 program or school support program that supports teachers and children in the classroom.
4. Increase parent involvement in literacy activities.

Implement a Schoolwide Staff Development Program in the Language Arts

Staff members have a diverse knowledge of reading. Many teachers have not had a language arts class since their undergraduate years. Most teachers update their learning through district inservices, conferences, professional readings, and classroom experience. Individually these methods are worthwhile and beneficial, however, as a collective staff, they are disjointed and eclectic at best.

Very few teachers actually know how to *teach* reading or have an understanding of literacy and literacy processes. In our undergraduate years, we usually learn how to assess and evaluate reading, and we learn about children's literature. Generally, there is also a language arts class given as a basic introduction to literacy. But, I don't recall ever having a class called *How to Teach Reading*. So, while many teachers are involved in wonderful language arts experiences on a daily basis, many of these experiences are not part of a bigger picture or understanding. They are isolated activities that are holistic in nature, but not part of a comprehensive, well-thought-out, thorough language arts program based upon demonstrated need.

Teachers need training. Intermediate teachers have expressed anxiety about their reading programs. Children reading independently in the intermediate grades require different reading strategies than primary emergent readers. A number of teachers in grades four through six also have children reading on primary levels that require emergent strategies, materials, and knowledge. Teachers at all levels need to be trained in all areas of language arts. It has been my experience that when I have worked with a child who has a very frustrated teacher concerned about their reading (for example, the child can't read, is LD, performs reversals, etc.), I have not found reason for any major concern. The child is usually just not developmentally ready for the materials. Rarely has there been a child with a true learning disability in this type of situation.

What we need is consistency in our knowledge, our language, and our understandings of what reading is and what learning is. If left alone, misconceptions can lead to a division among the staff as well as issues of prejudice, a self-fulfilling prophecy, hegemony, and teachers' misperceptions of their children and their children's literacies. These issues need to be discussed openly and honestly.

Establish Standardized Schoolwide Measures and Assessments that Support the School's Language Arts Program

There are two areas where this is of concern. The first is the dichotomy of teaching holistically and testing traditionally. The tests do not value the learner, do not reflect real literacies in authentic situations, and destroy a risk-free environment. The change in the way standardized measures are handled in the schools will set the tone for less stress on performance and make teaching and testing fair and understandable for the children and their parents.

The second inconsistency is evidenced between grade levels and in-house assessments. Because teachers' backgrounds are eclectic in both knowledge and application, there is little consistency in our language or evaluations regarding students. Some teachers use leveled books, some teachers use the reading series, some teachers do miscue, some teachers do IRIs. Teachers who use leveled books don't use the same leveled book series. Some teachers say the child is on level D, another teacher says the child is on level 8. The reading series reveals they are a Level III reader, and in class they're reading a Scholastic book leveled 2.5. What does it all mean? It means you have a variety of assessments to use to measure the child for that year. But, if you want your assessments to be used for the purpose of establishing growth across years, then the same assessments speaking the same language must be used at all grade levels. We do need to keep all of the different types of assessments we use in the classroom to inform us as teachers and allow us to become smarter about our students. But, we also need to determine what informal measures the school will use for determining growth over time. These need to be consistent. When Mrs. Jones sees that Tony is evaluated by the school as being a level 4 reader, she can assume that Tony performed as a level 4 reader on the leveled book series the school uses for consistent measures over time. This way, when everybody attends a meeting to discuss Tony's progress, they will not be talking apples and oranges.

Implement a Title 1 Program or School Support Program that Supports Teachers and Children in the Classroom

Rather than focusing on raising the individual test scores of every child, focus upon creating a literate environment and looking at the school overall. When supported, the classroom teachers are better equipped to provide individualized instruction within the context of the child's setting and life experiences. The school needs to create better schedules and materials, and provide more professionals that allow classroom teachers to:

- teach their class effectively
- implement one-to-one programs for children with the greatest needs
- implement instruction for children deemed below grade level, but not possessing the greatest needs

To accomplish this, language arts specialists or Title 1 teachers can:

- model language arts procedures in the classroom
- assist teachers in planning instruction
- assist teachers in the classroom
- have one-to-one meetings with teachers to discuss, accommodate, and establish classroom strategies and needs
- create a list of material resources for the teachers

Administrators, volunteers, language arts specialists, and Title 1 teachers can:

- focus heavily on the primary grades. Support kindergarten and first grade teachers with their literacy program, so there will be less problems as children progress through the higher grades. It is much easier and cheaper to teach these skills in the early years than to try to remediate them in later years.
- highlight and weave literacy throughout the school
- organize after school book clubs (book discussions after school)
- organize publishing clubs (writing workshops after school)
- create a school newspaper consisting only of children's writing, art, and so on
- provide author visits
- provide young author luncheons
- organize book battles
- organize storytelling clubs
- keep a section in the library for books and book reviews authored by classmates
- establish a principal's challenge[1]
- organize a storybook character dress-up day
- organize school debating teams, speech clubs, or demonstration days
- provide a school author's night where the children share their work
- establish penpals with another school
- provide schoolwide independent reading time (D.E.A.R.—Drop Everything and Read)

- implement and highlight listening and speaking as a significant part of the language arts program
- give teachers professional leave for attending a reading conference

Increase Parental Involvement in Literacy Activities

Three ways to increase parental involvement in literacy activities include:

- implementing parent/child evening story hours where the parent sees the strategies modeled as well as develops their own literacy. Children would not be able to attend these events without a parent.
- offering evening classes on the reading/writing process for parents with ideas on how to support their child at home.
- having parents work as school editors and book publishers.

I realize that the goals I have established here are long-term goals rather than short-term goals. There probably wouldn't be a huge overall improvement schoolwide in one year, or maybe even two years. But it would come. We have already seen the growth in Molly, Tony, Karen, and Kiev. We will only be able to do what is best for our children as long as we believe, remember, and trust that:

- all children learn differently and at different rates.
- all children come to school with diverse literacies and experiences.
- school literacy such as reading and writing is just one form of literacy.
- to support children in their literacy process, we must begin where the child is and work within the framework of the child's literacy strengths and competencies.
- reading and writing are interactive processes that support each other, therefore, they must be taught together to support the literacy processes.
- children learn to read and write by actually reading and writing.
- children will not involve themselves in an activity that they are poor at or do not enjoy.
- skills and strategies need to be taught in the context of the reading and writing process. Skills and strategies practiced separately are too abstract

and conditional for an emergent reader (in kindergarten or sixth grade) to assimilate.

- all areas of the language arts cuing systems (graphophonics, syntax, semantics, and pragmatics) need to be taught, and taught simultaneously within the context of the reading and writing process.
- different types of reading (fiction, non-fiction, letters, graphs, picture books, novels, etc.) develop different types of literacies and need to be included in the language arts program.
- children who perform below their peers often do so because they have had fewer experiences with print—not because there is something wrong with them. Once given adequate experiences with print, these children often begin working at their own potential; frequently catching up or surpassing their peers.
- the teaching of all areas of the language arts (reading, writing, listening, and speaking) is the central role and responsibility of the classroom teacher for all students in their class.
- all children can learn.

None of these approaches or practices violates any district's adopted reading program. Nor do they violate proper preparation for the federal, state specific, or district specific standardized assessments. They are by no means passive either. They are proactive positives that support the main tenets of education, i.e., to produce literate, independent readers.

Note

1. Poem of the month. The child that recites a poem to the principal gets a special pencil. These names are printed on chart paper and are hung in the library, cafeteria, or hall.

8

Final Thoughts

The success of our children will hinge more on our competencies and knowledge as teachers than by the competencies that our students are said to possess. Federal issues of mainstreaming and inclusion quickly become personal issues of knowledge, literacy, caring, and equity.

If we believe that all children can learn, then it is our job to create child-centered classrooms that allow them to do so. We need to get smarter about our teaching.

We must become knowledgeable about issues of literacy. We must become knowledgeable about the laws. And, most importantly, we must become knowledgeable about our children. We must utilize alternative curriculums and assessments that demonstrate the strengths (and needs) of our children. We must learn to create a negotiated curriculum based upon these demonstrated needs. And we must believe that it is important that we do so.

As teachers, we are the voice of our children. If we do not protect, advocate, and support our students in the classroom, who will? We cannot wait for school systems to become more receptive to children's and society's needs. We cannot wait for the proper amount of services and resources. We cannot wait for that one magical cure-all curriculum that will accommodate all needs.

It is our responsibility as professionals to create positive, rewarding learning opportunities within our classrooms for all that enter, today. We must continue to grow in our profession. We must keep our minds and doors open to foster increasing dialogue and changing perspectives. Today, by assuming a stance of advocacy, we have the opportunity, responsibility, and power to transform the life of every single child in our class. It is our knowledge and use of that power that will determine their future and the future of our country. We have an awesome responsibility—let's take it one child at a time.

Glossary

ADC (Aid to Dependent Children): This poverty variable is often used as a predictor and/or indicator of children deemed at risk.

ADD (Attention Deficit Disorder): A disorder relating to focusing and maintaining attention.

ADHD (Attention Deficit Hyperactivity Disorder): ADD plus hyperactivity. Problems relating to restlessness, impulsivity, and inattention.

At Risk: A child is deemed at risk if their prospects for success are considered marginal.

Child Study: Mandatory team of professionals that make decisions regarding a special education student's academic career.

EMH (Educably Mentally Handicapped): A child with a low IQ (2–3 standard deviations below the mean) who is able to learn and function adequately within society.

ESOL (English for/to Speakers of Other Languages): A child is generally referred for ESOL if they do not speak, write, read, or understand English, and their native language is not English.

FAPE (Free Appropriate Public Education): Section 504 states that all children are entitled to a free appropriate public education regardless of their disability.

IASA 94: Federal law that provides resources to schools in support of their efforts to help reach high standards. Oversees such programs as Title 1.

IDEA 97 (Individuals with Disabilities Education Act): The federal document that governs special education.

IEP (Individual Educational Program): The legal document that establishes baseline criteria as well as goals and procedures for the special education student.

Inclusion: The process and practice of educating students with disabilities in the general education classroom of their neighborhood school.

LD (Learning Disabled): A generic term referring to a heterogeneous group of disorders that is manifested in difficulties of listening, speaking, reading, writing, and/or math.

LEP (Limited English Proficiency): Typically bilingual children with a restricted understanding or use of written and spoken English.

LRE (Least Restrictive Environment): Section 504 states that every child, regardless of disability, must receive a free appropriate education in their least restrictive environment. If the regular classroom setting can physically and socially accommodate a child's needs, then that setting becomes the least restrictive environment.

Mainstream: When a child receives some, but not all, of their instruction in a regular classroom setting. Partial Inclusion.

OCR (Office of Civil Rights): Duties include overseeing Section 504 complaints and compliance.

Section 504: Section 504 of the Americans with Disabilities Act. The civil rights act that protects the constitutional rights of all persons of disability.

Section B (of IDEA 97): Contains the federal requirements regarding IEPs.

Title 1: Covered under IASA 94, Title 1 is a program established to help children of low economic status succeed in school. Formally called Chapter 1.

ZPD (Zone of Proximal Development [Vygotsky, 1978]): As related to this text, it refers to starting a child at their developmental and conceptual level, both academically and socially, as opposed to where the curriculum says they should be.

Index